S0-AXI-847

"Never losing his seasoned reporter's eye for detail, Aikman steps back to develop a wide-angle view of history and addresses a burning issue for America. A signal contribution to the current debate on the real state of the Union."

Os Guinness, author of *A Free People's Suicide*

"Readers searching for a succinct overview of the Christian role in America's past and present will relish David Aikman's balanced assessments and mellifluous prose."

Dr. Marvin Olasky, editor-in-chief, *World*

"In this stimulating book, David Aikman deftly assesses America's religious heritage and the possible consequences should Americans turn away from that heritage. From the founding of the early American colonies to contemporary trends in media and university life, Aikman offers an excellent introduction to a range of vital issues that have helped spawn today's culture wars."

Thomas S. Kidd, associate professor of history at Baylor University and author of *Patrick Henry: First Among Patriots*

"David Aikman's excellent book comes amid strenuous arguments about whether the United States is or was a Christian country and whether it could or should be one. These debates often ignore the complexity of Christianity's varying role in our history and are notably vague about what it might actually mean for America to be Christian. In this setting *One Nation without God?* clarifies the key issues through a lucid, spirited, and evenhanded overview of Christianity's role in American history and its possible futures. It is necessary reading."

Paul Marshall, author and senior fellow at the Hudson Institute's Center for Religious Freedom

Other Books by David Aikman

Hope: The Heart's Great Quest

Great Souls: Six Who Changed a Century

Jesus in Beijing: How Christianity Is Transforming China and Changing the Global Balance of Power

A Man of Faith: The Spiritual Journey of George W. Bush

Billy Graham: His Life and Influence

The Delusion of Disbelief: How the New Atheism Is a Threat to Your Life, Liberty, and Pursuit of Happiness

The Mirage of Peace: Understanding the Never-Ending Conflict in the Middle East

Awaken the Dragon: A Richard Ireton Novel

When the Almond Tree Blossoms

ONE NATION WITHOUT GOD?

The Battle for Christianity in an Age of Unbelief

DAVID AIKMAN

BakerBooks
a division of Baker Publishing Group
Grand Rapids, Michigan

Published by Baker Books
a division of Baker Publishing Group
P.O. Box 6287, Grand Rapids, MI 49516-6287
www.bakerbooks.com

Printed in the United States of America

Library of Congress Cataloging-in-Publication Data is on file at the Library of Congress, Washington, DC.

Scripture quotations are from the King James Version of the Bible.

The internet addresses, email addresses, and phone numbers in this book are accurate at the time of publication. They are provided as a resource. Baker Publishing Group does not endorse them or vouch for their content or permanence.

Published in association with the Barbara Casey Literary Agency, Trion, Georgia.

12 13 14 15 16 17 18 7 6 5 4 3 2 1

In loving memory of my mother, Joy Aikman (1914–1992),
a woman of unlimited compassion and joy who,
at the age of 17, wrote the following lines:

Have you walked into a village church and felt the quietness
And knelt down in the stillness for a prayer?
Have you sat there in the mistiness and straightened out your thoughts—
And known that someone else was sitting there?
Have you walked with aching feet along a dusty country lane
And smelt the scent of newly mown hay?
Have you listened to a river as it sings across the stones
And laughs and cries along the way?
But when the wind is blowing and you stand high on a hill
And feel you're right above the greed and strife—
That is when you're happy—when you know you love the world—
When you know that God is God—Yes, that is life.

Contents

1

Not a Christian Nation?

The Battle for Our National Identity

The first trumpet blast came from the president of the United States. It was April 6, 2009, less than three months after Barack Obama was sworn in, hand on a Bible, on the western front of the Capitol, promising to "defend the Constitution of the United States." Now in Turkey to conclude a five-nation European tour, Obama was standing with his host, Turkish president Abdullah Gul, at a podium in Ankara's ornate Cankaya Palace answering questions from Turkish, American, and foreign reporters. A Turkish reporter asked him what he intended to do to improve US-Turkish relations, which, the reporter said, had deteriorated under the administration of George W. Bush. Obama's answer was that the United States and Turkey might demonstrate a new model of cooperation. "And I've said before," the president noted, "that one of the great strengths of the United States is—although as I mentioned, we have a very large Christian population—we do not consider ourselves a Christian nation or a Jewish nation or a Muslim nation; we consider ourselves a nation of citizens who are bound by ideals and a set of values."[1]

NOT A CHRISTIAN NATION?

The blogosphere quickly hummed with these words and excited some disapproving discussion. "He has done the country a lot of harm this week, harm that I fear is going to come back and bite us just like misunderstanding our enemies bought us 9-11," a reader named Daneen commented on the site LonelyConservative.com.[2] Another snippy response came from blogger Debbie Schlussel: "Hmmm . . . I guess Christmas and New Year's Day should be crossed off the federal holiday schedule."[3] New Year's Day is a federal holiday, though it is not technically part of the Christian Christmas liturgy.

Obama's remarks in Turkey were not the first time he had made this assertion. In June 2007, while still a US senator but having already announced his bid for the presidency, he responded by email to the Christian Broadcasting Network's senior national correspondent David Brody with the comment, "Whatever we once were, we're no longer just a Christian nation. We are also a Jewish nation, a Muslim nation, a Buddhist nation, and a Hindu nation, and a nation of non-believers."[4] This led some critics to charge that by the time he made his remarks in Turkey, Obama had, in effect, become even more radical in his rejection of America's Christian heritage. "Note the progression," John Eidsmoe observed on the website of *The New American* magazine. "In 2007, he said we are no longer 'just' a Christian nation. Now, in 2009, he says we 'do not consider ourselves a Christian nation' at all."[5]

Other personalities, speaking on the Fox News channel, were even more hostile. Newt Gingrich, the former GOP speaker of the house, asserted that Obama "was fundamentally misleading about the nature of America." Fox News anchor Sean Hannity said that he was "offended" and that Obama was "out of touch with the principles that have made this country great." Karl Rove, former senior political advisor under George W. Bush, suggested that Obama had denied the reality that America was founded on faith, though he in fact virtually echoed Obama's own comments. "Yeah, look," he added, "America is a nation built on faith. I mean, we can be Christian, we can be Jew, we can be Mormon, we can be, you know, any variety of things. We're a country that prizes faith and believes that we are endowed by our Creator with certain inalienable rights; among them are life, liberty, and the pursuit of happiness." As for Fox News host Megyn Kelly, she wondered if Obama had "step[ped] on a political landmine." She said, implying she agreed with the idea, that Obama "was obviously just pandering. He was in this Muslim nation saying, look, we're not a Christian country—and by the way, this is not the first time he's said this. He gave a speech back in June of 2006, according to our records, where he said exactly this, and then again he repeated it the following year."[6]

Other internet comments were even more pointed. On the conservative website Red State, Warner Todd Huston headlined his opinion piece rhetorically by asking, "What are we if NOT a Christian nation?" He said Obama was simply "ingratiating himself with Muslim audiences."[7]

Yet many commentators strongly supported President Obama's assertion, and did so skillfully. Michael Lind, a policy director at the New America Foundation, elaborated a thoughtful argument that conservative critics of Obama had conflated Christianity and natural rights liberalism. Lind argued that automatically identifying the "Creator" in the Declaration of Independence with the "personal god of the Abrahamic religions" was wrong because the ideas of natural rights and the social contract inherited by the founders had their origins in Hobbes, Gassendi, and Locke, who themselves drew on themes founded in Greek and Roman philosophy. "President Obama . . . is right," Lind argued. "The American republic, as distinct from the American population, is not post-Christian because it was never Christian."[8]

Randall Balmer, professor of American religious history at Barnard College, an editor for *Christianity Today* magazine, and an Episcopal priest, argued, albeit somewhat defensively, in the *Huffington Post* that "America is not a Christian nation and evangelicals are not hard right."[9] It is worth pointing out that just prior to Obama's election as president, one of the *New York Times* bestsellers was Jim Wallis's *God's Politics*.[10] Wallis is a prominent spokesman for what is sometimes called "the Christian left" and has taken a generally left-leaning political position on both domestic and international issues for three decades or so. He was a prominent opponent of Operation Desert Storm, the first Gulf War to liberate Kuwait from Iraq, and a vociferous critic of anything slightly suggestive of Christian nationalism.

MEACHAM ON THE DECLINE OF CHRISTIAN AMERICA

The argument over President Obama's rather abrupt declaration that America was not really a Christian nation might have gradually receded from people's minds except for one of those intriguing coincidences historians like to mull over. Within hours of Obama's comments in Turkey, a *Newsweek* cover luridly emblazoned with a cross-shaped red-on-black headline, "The Decline and Fall of Christian America," appeared on American and European newsstands. As if Americans were unaware of the spiritual issues of the day, the issue was dated April 13 and appeared the week before the Christian celebration of Easter.

Written by then managing editor Jon Meacham, the *Newsweek* piece made it clear that the headline itself was not such a bad statement. "While we remain a nation decisively shaped by religious faith," Meacham wrote, "our politics and our culture are, in the main, less influenced by movements and arguments of an explicitly Christian character than they were even five years ago. I think this is a good thing—good for our political culture, which, as the American Founders saw, is complex and charged enough without attempting to compel or coerce religious belief or observance. It is good for Christianity, too, in that many Christians are rediscovering the virtues of a separation of church and state that protects what Roger Williams, who founded Rhode Island as a haven for religious dissenters, called 'the garden of the church' from 'the wilderness of the world.'"[11]

To his credit, Meacham acknowledged Christian Americans who differed profoundly with him in this assessment. One of them, extensively quoted in the story, was R. Albert Mohler Jr., president of the Southern Baptist Theological Seminary in Louisville, Kentucky. Meacham quoted Mohler as agreeing that there had been a major shift in American life away from support for Christianity but not as approving of this shift. Mohler had lamented that "a remarkable culture-shift [had] taken place around us. The most basic contours of American culture have been radically altered. The so-called Judeo-Christian consensus of the last millennium has given way to a post-modern, post-Christian, post-Western cultural crisis which threatens the very heart of our culture," Meacham wrote. The "culture shift" that grieved Mohler included the near-doubling since 1990 of the number of Americans claiming "no religious affiliation," as *Newsweek* noted, from 8 to 15 percent. Mohler told Meacham, "Clearly, there is a new narrative, a post-Christian narrative, that is animating large portions of this society."[12]

A *Newsweek* poll accompanying Meacham's report buttressed his argument. It showed that in 2009, the first year of Obama's presidency, fewer people said they regarded the United States as a "Christian nation" than did so when George W. Bush was president (62 percent in 2009 versus 69 percent in 2008). Moreover, two-thirds of the public (68 percent) said they thought religion was "losing influence" in American society, while only 19 percent said they thought religion's influence was on the rise. Perhaps even more disturbing for those troubled by Meacham's analysis, the proportion of Americans who thought that religion could "answer all or most of today's problems" was now at a historic low of 48 percent. During the preceding George W. Bush and Clinton years, that figure had never dropped below 58 percent, according to *Newsweek*.[13]

Meacham, an Episcopalian of more liberal theological and political persuasion than most evangelicals in the United States, seemed in the *Newsweek* piece eager to show that by referring to the "decline" of Christianity in America, he was referring largely to the diminishing profile of the "religious right," that segment of America's evangelicals who, at least since the late 1970s, had played a conspicuous role in our nation's politics. Meacham argued that "being *less* Christian" did not necessarily mean that America was "post-Christian." After all, as is clear in the American Religious Identification Survey (ARIS) conducted by researchers at Trinity College in Hartford, Connecticut, one-third of all Americans identified themselves as "born-again," a term specifically expressing a personal commitment to the Christian faith. The results of their 2008 survey led the ARIS authors to note that "trends . . . suggest a movement towards more conservative beliefs and particularly to a more 'evangelical' outlook among Christians."[14]

Meacham claimed that his assessment of the end of Christian America had derived from reflections on what he described as four decades of a "ferocious" struggle by the Christian right to undo the damage to the American Christian heritage that, in their view, had been wrought by the 1962 Engel v. Vitale Supreme Court decision banning government-composed prayer in public schools. In Meacham's view, the Christian right in America longed "to engineer a return to what it believed was a Christian America of yore."[15]

Mohler, for all of his evangelistic leanings, appeared to show some sympathy for Meacham's assessment, almost nostalgically lamenting what he feared would result from Christianity's slow erosion in American national life. Choosing his words with the precision honed by years as an administrator and teacher at the Southern Baptist Theological Seminary, Mohler told Meacham,

> The moral teachings of Christianity have exerted an incalculable influence on Western civilization. As those moral teachings fade into cultural memory, a secularized morality takes their place. Once Christianity is abandoned by a significant portion of the population, the moral landscape necessarily changes. For the better part of the 20th century, the nations of Western Europe led the way in the abandonment of Christian

> commitments. Christian moral reflexes and moral principles gave way to the loosening grip of a Christian memory. Now even that Christian memory is absent from the lives of millions.[16]

Mohler may well be correct in his assessment of the erosion of the Christian consensus in Western society, but the triumph of secularism may not be the end of the story.

CHRISTIANITY ON THE ROPES

If Christianity really was on the ropes, at least in terms of moral influence on society, as Mohler worried, what on earth had brought this about? A rich debate ensued online. For Presbyterian Darryl G. Hart, founder of the staunchly conservative Old Life Theological Society and its website, Oldlife.org, the fault lay in the eagerness of some Christians to try to use state power to promote Christianity, a temptation well documented in the book by Cal Thomas and Ed Dobson, *Blinded by Might*.[17] To buttress his position, Hart quoted fellow Presbyterian T. David Gordon as saying,

> If there is any real evidence of the decline of Christianity in the West, the evidence resides precisely in the eagerness of so many professing Christians to employ the state to advance the Christian religion. That is, if [Christian lay theologian and unconventional philosopher Jacques] Ellul's theory is right, the evidence of the decline of Christianity resides not in the presence of other religions (including secularism) in our culture, but in the emphasis by judges like Judge Roy Moore, a determined supporter of physical symbols like displays of the Ten Commandments in public places, in the hand-wringing over the phrase "under God" in the Pledge of

> Allegiance, and the whining about the "war on Christmas." If professing Christians believe our religion is advanced by the power of the state rather than by the power of the Spirit, by coercion rather than by example and moral suasion, then perhaps Christianity is indeed in decline.[18]

Hart's diagnosis of Christianity's decline in the United States was that Christians were simply far too political for their own good and for the good of Christianity in general. Hart noted, "But here is my concern: where in scripture are we told we have a 'right' to preach the gospel? I only see the categories of 'command,' as in, 'Go therefore and make disciples of all nations, baptizing them in the name of the Father and of the Son and of the Holy Spirit, teaching them to observe all that I have commanded you.' I don't see things like '. . . and make sure the powers that be leave you unhampered to do what I command you.'" Hart went on,

> We are commanded to be faithful and obedient to God to preach the gospel. "Rights" seem to imply that the preaching of the gospel is somehow for us to enjoy for our sake instead of doing it for the sake of others. If that is true, I don't see what difference it makes if you are representing me or the ACLU, because my concern isn't so much whether I have a right to my beliefs and practices (and that they are being protected) but rather if I am being faithful and obedient to what God has commanded.[19]

A similar, bracing view of the *Newsweek* analysis was conveyed by *Washington Post* writer E. J. Dionne: "Something is changing, and that change will strengthen rather than weaken the Christian church over the long run." Dionne said he thought that for the previous twenty-five years Christianity had been defined in a very conservative manner and "allied with a single political party."[20] This prompted one blogger to comment,

> On one level, Christians should be concerned about the "Decline and Fall of Christian America." Christians always want people to embrace the Gospel and should lament the fact that fewer people identify themselves with Christian faith. Perhaps this "decline and fall" might prompt Christians to put more effort into doing the work of the Church—fulfilling the Great Commission and loving God and neighbor. On the other hand, Christians should not be scared by these demographic developments. In fact, they just might do the Church some good.[21]

Despite the resounding response of approval for the *Newsweek* message about Christianity in America in many quarters, some readers flatly contested its conclusions. "As Easter 2009 approaches," wrote Douglas V. Gibbs on the website *Canada Free Press*, "the claim by the humanistic left that not only are we not a Christian nation, but never [were], becomes more and more rooted in their rabid fantasies. The reality of history is not only becoming ignored by some, but is literally being rewritten by those that hope to benefit from the death of religion, specifically Christianity, in America."[22] Blogging on another website, Todd Strandberg began a post with the impish heading, "The End of Christian America? Not Really." Christianity was in "good demographic shape," he argued, with the number of self-identified Christians up from a 1990 figure of 151.2 million to a 2009 figure of 173.4 million. "To have *Newsweek* and CNN predicting the end of Christian America," he said sardonically, "is like the dinosaurs telling the cockroaches that their days are numbered." He referred untactfully—and perhaps irrelevantly—to *Newsweek*'s decline in readers over previous years as essentially discrediting the magazine's reporting.[23]

As American Christians began to reflect on Meacham's assessment in *Newsweek* of the decline of Christianity, however, many who had for years kept a close eye on developments in culture and society began to express a view that seemed to reinforce Meacham's. One such person was Christian radio commentator Hank Hanegraaff, popularly known as "The Bible Answer Man," who has his own daily program answering questions from listeners about the Bible and Christian topics in general. Said Hanegraaff, "I have a very pessimistic outlook with respect to American evangelicals. I think America is going to look like Europe in the near future. I think we are going to look very much like Europe." He added, "The crux of this issue is a false dichotomy. . . . A sense of the divine is a sense of awe when we look at the universe. I think it is akin to the false dichotomy of the Enlightenment. I think we should have a reasonable truth."[24] The "false dichotomy" of which Hanegraaff was speaking is a view that an individual person might have a "sense of the divine" in his perceptions of the beauty of the universe but be unable to articulate that in a way that accorded with reason.

A REASONABLE TRUTH

The question is, however, who decides what is "reasonable truth"? Since about 2006, people of faith in the United States seem to have been under a general assault from the writings, debates, and lectures of people who collectively comprise a phenomenon known as "the New Atheism." Led by Oxford University ethologist and evolutionary biologist Richard Dawkins, the four bestselling authors who lead the New Atheism movement are sometimes referred to as "The Four Horsemen" (from a passage in the biblical book of Revelation about "the four horsemen of the apocalypse"). Between them, they've sold more than a million books. Each of the books—published in 2006 and 2007—took an aggressively hostile attitude toward faith and toward Christian belief in particular.[25] One of the more prominent atheistic writers was British-born Christopher Hitchens, a pugnacious and sometimes caustically aggressive writer and television commentator who tragically died of cancer of the esophagus in 2011.

MOVING FROM THE DIMINISHED CHURCH TO THE DEFENSIVE CHURCH

Christianity in America has been under sustained attack before, of course, including about a century ago during what is sometimes called "the golden age of freethought," between approximately 1856 and World War I. One of the most prominent orators favoring agnosticism was Robert G. Ingersoll.[26] Others have thought the "golden age" might have extended to the late 1920s and 1930s. At that time several skeptics took advantage of the intellectual bludgeoning suffered by American fundamentalists in the wake of the "Scopes Monkey Trial" over evolution in Dayton, Tennessee. We will deal with the Scopes trial in greater detail in chapter 4.

The difference between earlier periods of assault on faith by atheists and the recent period of American history described by the *Newsweek* article is that in the earlier periods, intellectual attacks on faith by atheists were not in general accompanied by an aggressive campaign by secularists to eliminate from public life as many public manifestations of Christian belief as possible.

According to the website of the Alliance Defense Fund, a legal alliance aimed at defending Christian religious liberty through strategy, training, funding, and litigation, "For decades, the American Civil Liberties Union (ACLU) and other radical anti-Christian groups have been on a mission to eliminate public expression of our nation's faith and heritage. By influencing the government, filing lawsuits, and spreading the myth of the so-called 'separation of church and state,' the opposition has been successful at forcing its leftist agenda on Americans."[27]

The ACLU was founded in 1920 by Roger Nash Baldwin, Walter Nelles, and others as an outgrowth of an earlier organization that campaigned against United States participation in World War I and defended conscientious objectors. On its website, the organization asserts that it is "our nation's guardian of liberty" and that among the rights of Americans it fights to defend are First Amendment rights, including "freedom of religion."[28] The website further asserts, "The goal of the ACLU's work on freedom of religion and belief is to guarantee that all are free to follow and practice their faith—or no faith at all—without governmental influence or interference."[29] But within many Christian circles there is a belief that the ACLU is intent on removing public expressions of Christian belief that may be offensive to atheists or agnostics.

In fact, the ACLU has repeatedly found itself in litigation against organizations like the Alliance Defense Fund over the issue of the right of individuals or groups to express religious convictions in settings where some people might disagree with them. The ACLU has frequently found itself in alliance with another organization whose purpose is quite specifically to propagandize Americans against any religious influence, whether guaranteed by the First Amendment or not. That particular group is the Freedom from Religion Foundation, based in Madison, Wisconsin. The FFRF, as it is sometimes referred to, was founded in 1976 by a mother and daughter team, Anne Nicol Gaylor and Annie Laurie Gaylor. The organization is currently cochaired by the daughter and her husband, Dan Barker, a former Pentecostal minister.

The website is interesting in its somewhat self-congratulatory description of the group ("the largest freethought association in North America") and its determination to discourage as many people as possible from having any sort of religious faith, Christian or otherwise. It touts an "out of the closet" campaign, featuring photographs of private citizens who wish to be identified publicly as atheists. These photographs are then blown up to a size large enough to decorate sizeable chunks of city buses in different parts of the United States. Not surprisingly, a very large number of them identify themselves as coming from Madison, where FFRF is based. "I have faith in people, not in a god. I don't need a god to be happy," says the statement next to Melanie, who describes herself as "a recovering Catholic, living for the moment." It is interesting that on the FFRF website—and presumably in most, if not all, of their literature—"god" is deliberately written in lowercase. As small-minded as this orthographic practice might seem today, it was prominently employed by Lenin and the Bolsheviks soon after the Bolshevik Revolution in Russia in 1917 as one of the first reforms intended to change the ways of thinking of ordinary Russians. In the Bolshevik case, what might have been considered at the outset a case of orthographic pettiness evolved into one of the most vicious antireligious movements in history.

Katie, twenty-three, also from Madison, is photographed in a T-shirt with the words "godless goddess" on the front of it and holding a plate of cookies. "I like biking, baking, and sleeping in on Sundays," she says. Bob Hinds, a middle-aged male also from Madison, is quoted as saying, "Being kind with an open mind is my religion." The FFRF has actually paid for its own monument at Lake Hypatia, Alabama, to "atheists in foxholes," a sort of tongue-in-cheek riposte to the frequently cited adage "There are no atheists in foxholes." The monument reads, "In memory of ATHEISTS IN FOXHOLES and the countless FREETHINKERS who have served this country with honor and distinction."

In fact, the FFRF spends a great deal of its time—and no doubt much of its money—fighting lawsuits to drive religion, and especially Christianity, out of the American public space. Matt Staver, director of the Liberty Counsel, an organization that fights in court to defend Christian religious expression from attack by secularist groups, says that the FFRF "strategizes on how to attack Christian viewpoints and Christian expression. They take Christian expressions and mimic them with different words. They put out bumper stickers. They are not a separation of church and state operation."[30]

Many of the suits might seem absurd to the average American. The FFRF, for example, prevented a city hall in Green Bay, Wisconsin, from displaying a crèche in its entrance and also successfully prevented the Cherry Creek School District in Denver, Colorado, from, to use FFRF's own words, "illegally urging that children spend an hour a week at a religious institution." The program encouraged parents to promote "40 development assets" as a way to ensuring that their children's lives enrich their "family, school and community." Families were told that asset-rich children were likely to be successful in their lives. But asset 19 was "Religious Community—Young person spends one or more hours per week in activities in a religious institution." The

FFRF argued, successfully, that "adoption, promotion, endorsement, approval and publicizing of Development Asset 19" by the school district "constituted an establishment of religion in violation of the First Amendment to the Constitution," as well as violating the prohibition against teaching sectarian tenets or doctrines found in the Colorado Constitution.[31]

Other victories celebrated by the FFRF include the fencing-off of a statue of Jesus in a Wisconsin public park with "Christ, Guide Us on Our Way" at the base of the statue. Atheists and agnostics had argued that they were offended by the idea that the statue was on public property. The city of Marshfield was ordered to erect a conspicuous sign on the surrounding fence that read, "PRIVATE PARK. This enclosed property is not owned or maintained by the city of Marshfield, nor does the city endorse the religious expression thereon." Well, the good citizens of Wisconsin are reliably informed that the state and city authorities don't want anyone to be under the illusion that they might have a sympathetic attitude towards religion.

But the FFRF lost a case that could have had national repercussions had the decision gone the other way. A First Circuit Court judge rejected an FFRF attempt to have the phrase "under God" removed from the Pledge of Allegiance in New Hampshire schools. Judge Sandra Lea Lynch said, "In reciting the Pledge, students promise fidelity to our flag and nation, not to any particular God, faith, or church."[32]

PUSHING BACK

The faith community in the United States is well defended in these court cases by several Christian legal organizations, such as the Alliance Defense Fund, the Rutherford Institute, the

Liberty Counsel, the American Center for Law and Justice, and Wallbuilders, a Texas-based organization dedicated to protecting Americans' awareness of their historical connections with devout Christians throughout the nation's story. On the website of the Alliance Defense Fund is a statement that reads, "The ACLU's attacks on religious freedom are more serious and widespread than you may realize. In courtrooms and schoolrooms, offices and shops, public buildings and even churches . . . those who believe in God are increasingly threatened, punished, and silenced."[33] The ADF says in another location on its website,

> For more than 50 years, the ACLU and other radical activist groups have attempted to eliminate public expression of our nation's faith and heritage. They have done this through fear, intimidation, disinformation, and the filing of lawsuits (or threats of lawsuits) that would:
>
> - Eliminate Christian and historic faith symbols from government documents, buildings, and monuments
> - Ban public prayer in schools and at school functions
> - Deny Christians the right to use public facilities that are open to other groups
> - Prevent Christians from expressing their faith in the workplace
>
> Through attacks like these, the ACLU and its allies have sought to limit the spread and influence of the Gospel in the United States.[34]

Actually, the ADF and allied legal groups have won more cases than they have lost, but they are certainly kept busy. Among the horror stories brought out by the ADF is that of a woman in Houston threatened with arrest by the local police for handing out gospel tracts to children who knocked on her front door during Halloween. The policemen told her—erroneously—that this activity was illegal. The ADF worked to force the University of California, Los Angeles to permit a graduating student to thank Jesus Christ during her graduation ceremony. Too numerous to mention are the past court cases (invariably won by the ADF) that force schools to permit Christian clubs to operate on campus, outside of school hours, with the same rights and privileges as non-Christian clubs.

More worrying for the ADF and all concerned about freedom-of-conscience issues have been decisions by educational institutions to force enrolled students to accept, and even to endorse, homosexual behavior. The ADF brought a case against Augusta State University in Georgia for essentially forcing a Christian student, Jen Keeton, then twenty-four, either to abandon her Christian beliefs and to attend compulsory "sensitivity training" or to face expulsion from the school. Keeton said that her Christian beliefs defined her attitude toward homosexual behavior. Keeton had asserted, both inside and outside the classroom, that she considered homosexual behavior (not orientation as such) a matter of "behavioral choice," not a state of being. The college authorities, until challenged in court, insisted that Keeton attend a "remediation" program, a sort of thought reform program similar to those concocted during the Chinese Cultural Revolution, in which she would be forced to attend "sensitivity training" on homosexuality and to be an observer of—and then report on—a "gay pride" event. The Keeton case is currently pending in federal district court. The school's argument was unconsciously ironic. It expelled Keeton, then argued that the case was moot because she was no longer a student.

In a similar case, a student at Eastern Michigan State University, Julea Ward, was expelled from the counseling program at the college on March 12, 2009, for refusing to change her religious convictions and endorse homosexual behavior. Since the college is a publicly funded institution, many state legislators were understandably alarmed that a public educational institution would impose what many people regarded as a religious test for students. David French, senior counsel for the ADF, commented, "When a public university has a prerequisite of affirming homosexual behavior as morally good in order to obtain a degree, the school is stepping over the legal line." Ward was also told that the only way she could avoid expulsion was a "remediation" program—in other words, thought reform. The case is pending an appeal. Interestingly, the Michigan State Attorney General, the highest legal official in the state, filed an amicus (i.e., supporting) brief on the side of Ward's defenders, the Alliance Defense Fund.

Jay Sekulow is president of the American Center for Law and Justice, which litigates frequently over issues of religious freedom. Commenting on the number of cases he sees that require aggressive litigation to preserve First Amendment rights of "free exercise" of religion, Sekulow was pessimistic about social trends. He said, "You have a confluence of two things—a secularist agenda and militant political convictions—that has brought together in a mutual alliance militant secularists and even Islamists." The opponents of Christianity, Sekulow argued, had "not had much success in the courtroom. But they have had great success in the court of public opinion."[35]

PUBLIC OPINION

People disagree, of course, on what "the court of public opinion" means, but it surely includes the world of Hollywood and entertainment, reporting by many news organizations, and the academic world. We have already seen how the academic world is increasingly hostile toward orthodox Christian positions. Hollywood in recent years has been as averse to portraying Christians sympathetically as college campuses often have been to treating Christian ideas with fairness. Many elite media publications, particularly on both coasts, have also been hostile to Christian positions.

The movie industry's hostility to traditional American religious views was first well reported in 1993 in Michael Medved's book *Hollywood vs. America*, in which Medved argued, among other things, that much of Hollywood's vendetta against Christianity is driven by ideology, not profits.[36] Other critics have demonstrated beyond reasonable doubt that movies with strong anti-Christian themes consistently do less well at the box office than movies with upbeat content and with a generally favorable view of Christianity. The research staff of Dr. Ted Baehr, founder and chairman of Christian Film and Television, watched and analyzed 750 movies between 2002 and 2004. Movies with "strong moral messages" (not necessarily Christian) earned about four to seven times as much money, on average, as movies with content blatantly in opposition to traditional Christian morality.[37] In short, the financial bottom line in Hollywood seems to carry less weight than the ideological position of the power brokers in Hollywood.

"There is no doubt that the fissure is growing much, much deeper," says Rev. Jim Garlow, senior pastor of San Diego's Skyline Church. "If we don't have a revival we are in for persecution." Garlow's church has sometimes required police protection because of Garlow's role in supporting California's Proposition 8 (the California ballot proposition and state constitutional amendment declaring that only marriages between a man and a woman should be legally recognized by the state, which was passed by 52.4 percent of California voters but then overturned in federal district court). Garlow says that opponents of Christianity, especially within the gay community and on liberal-leaning television networks like MSNBC, have been vitriolic in their opposition. The federal Ninth Circuit Court of Appeals recently upheld the ruling that found Proposition 8 unconstitutional, and the case is expected to end up before the US Supreme Court.

"I definitely think we have sunk to a new level," Garlow says. "Look at [the Old Testament book of] Isaiah 5:20. They call 'good,' 'bad' and 'bad,' 'good.' I think we are seeing a sign. The left doesn't even stop to care whether we are transgressing the First Amendment. Civil discourse is almost impossible. The radical left is incapable of civil discourse. [Television anchors like] Rachel Maddow and Keith Olbermann are just vitriolic."[38] Jay Sekulow agrees. "The media bias issue is increasingly becoming a central one," he says. "The left is much more vicious, making fun of people. What is said about Christians could not be said about Muslims."[39] Of course, people on the right can be vindictive too, but aside from Fox News, there is much less visible presence of conservatives in the general American news media.

The appearance that Christianity in America has been under direct attack from parts of the judiciary, from the academic community, from Hollywood, and from the media has prompted a number of people to write books that raise the cultural alarm. David Limbaugh's *Persecution: How Liberals Are Waging a War Against Christianity* was a bestseller in 2006. A more recent volume is *America's War on Christianity* by Brad O'Leary.[40] Limbaugh's contention that the culture of the United States is moving decisively against the public expression of Christian belief is backed up by a variety of legal, academic, and journalistic incidents that he cites.

Almost more shocking than anything cited on the websites of the Alliance Defense Fund or Sekulow's American Center for Law and Justice is an occasion in May 1995 when Judge Samuel B. Kent, United States judge for the Southern District of Texas, declared from the bench that anyone uttering the word "Jesus" during a high school graduation ceremony would be arrested and incarcerated for six months. For good measure, the judge added, "Anyone who violates these orders, no kidding, is going to wish that he or she had died as a child when this court gets through with it." Mindful of the need to be equally repressive to all religions, the judge added that any prayer offered "must not refer to a specific deity by name, whether it be Jesus, Buddha, Mohammed, the Great God Sheba or anyone else."[41] In reality, it might have been Judge Kent who wished that he had experienced a different childhood. Imprisoned on charges of sexual harassment of female co-workers, he was indicted, went to jail, and then was impeached in 2009 by the United States House of Representatives and stripped of all his retirement benefits.

Kent's intemperate haranguing of graduating high school students was matched by what could be judged as one of the more egregious journalistic lapses of recent decades. When Dylan Klebold and Eric Harris massacred twelve classmates and one teacher at Columbine High School in Colorado before taking their own lives in April 1999, one of the most horrifying aspects of the shootings was their apparent deliberate targeting of outspoken Christians among the students. Though the Christian martyrdom aspect of the deaths of Cassie Bernall and

Rachel Scott were well publicized (Klebold and Harris reportedly specifically asked whether their victims were Christians before shooting them) at the time of the incident, *Time* magazine devoted twenty pages to a cover story on the shootings without once mentioning videos made before the shootings in which Klebold and Harris revealed the depth of their hatred, specifically, of Christians. In one of them, Klebold faces the camera and asks, "What would Jesus do? What would I do?" He points an imaginary gun at the camera and says, "Boosh!" In the background Harris is heard saying, "Yeah, I love Jesus. I love Jesus. Shut the f--- up. Go Romans. Thank God they crucified that a--hole."[42]

Time's lapse in the Columbine report may have had a variety of explanations. Harder to brush aside, however, are examples of the media's sometimes downright hostility in their attitude toward America's Christians. When *Washington Post* reporter Michael Weisskopf was writing about Christian conservative supporters of the Christian Coalition in 1993, he casually opined that Christians were "largely poor, uneducated, and easy to command." The comment was a public relations disaster for the *Washington Post*, which for a time required full-time staffers just to handle the faxed bank statements, photocopies of college degrees, and other paraphernalia that flowed into the paper as proof of how wrong Weisskopf had been. In fairness to Weisskopf, whom I knew personally as a talented and courageous reporting colleague a few years earlier in China, there was almost certainly no malice in the statement. Weisskopf simply reflected an ignorance of and indifference to America's Christians that is all too typical of many American reporters.

Brad O'Leary's book focuses not only on cases of journalistic malfeasance but also on additional instances of legal overreach in suppressing Christianity in public. He draws attention to the need for America's Christian legacy to be assessed accurately and the need to fight against what he considers a whitewashing of America's history books.

Other worriers about cultural decline, however, have noted positive statements about Christianity's role in society from members of the judiciary who otherwise have had a reputation for seeming always to prefer the liberal (and usually anti-Christian) side of legal opinions. In Limbaugh's book, Supreme Court Justice William O. Douglas is cited as the author of an important Supreme Court ruling back in 1952, which held that schools may hold Bible study during the school day, providing no public funds are used, teachers in the Bible study program are not state-approved, and there is no coercion. Justice Douglas wrote,

> We are a religious people whose institutions presuppose a Supreme Being. . . . When the state encourages religious instruction or cooperates with religious authorities by adjusting the schedule of public events to sectarian needs, it then follows the best of our traditions. For it then respects the religious nature of our people and accommodates the public services to their spiritual needs. To hold that it may not would be to find in the Constitution a requirement that the government show a callous indifference to religious groups. That would be preferring those who believe in no religion over those who do believe. . . . But we find no constitutional requirement that makes it necessary for government to be hostile to religion and to throw its weight against efforts to widen the effective scope of religious influence. But it can close its doors or suspend its operations as those who want to repair to their religious sanctuary for worship of instruction. No more than that is undertaken here.[43]

Neither Limbaugh nor O'Leary, however, addresses a question that is perhaps just as important as the historical issue of the role of Christianity in American life. That question is this: Is there an actual falling away from traditional Christian belief among churchgoers and their offspring? If so, how significant is it in an overall examination of the role of Christianity in America?

2

Where Are the Christians in America?

Withdrawal vs. Retreat

If Americans have become worried about the state of public commitment to Christianity in the United States, they are not initially advised to look to the next rising generation, the so-called Millennials. These are young people who were born after 1980 and who began to come of age around the year 2000. Millennials have been studied almost as intensively as the baby boomer generation, that demographic hiccup in the twentieth century that resulted from the unusually high American birthrate between 1946 and 1964. Between those years, some 76 million Americans were born, in contrast to the years during World War II, when so many American men were serving in the military overseas that starting families was difficult, if not impossible, for America's young adults.

The baby boomer generation, which has included at least two US presidents (Bill Clinton and George W. Bush, born within less than two months of each other in 1946) and most of the prominent entertainers, actors, and politicians of our era, has cost the lives of many trees felled to satisfy the never-ending public curiosity about this generation. It was, above all, famous—or notorious, depending on your politics—for the groundswell of opposition among young people to the war in Vietnam in the 1960s and for the countercultural activities that will forever be associated with that decade: rock music, hippies, promiscuous sex, and political protest.

By contrast with their raucous elders, who were sometimes the parents of the Millennials, the generation of young people aged eighteen to twenty-nine who came of age after the year 2000 is much less rebellious and not really countercultural. However, they are in every sense children of postmodernism, which, as we shall see, is a philosophical attitude almost calculated to disengage its practitioners from any firm philosophical commitment and, it might be said, sometimes from reality itself.

THE PEW FORUM ON RELIGION AND PUBLIC LIFE

In February 2010 the Pew Forum on Religion and Public Life published one of the most thorough studies of who the Millennials are and what they believe—or don't believe—that has been produced so far. Titled *Millennials: A Portrait of Generation Next*, the report had the subtitle *Confident. Connected. Open to Change*. Based on a telephone survey conducted January 14–27, 2010, with a nationally representative sample of 2,020 adults, it reflects the fact that each generation of young Americans since the 1960s has been technologically more savvy than the preceding generation and in general is more sympathetic to the novelty of communication that high technology has created.[1] For example, a majority of Millennials thought that new technology had the effect of bringing people closer together, in contrast with only 44 percent of the "Silent" generation, Americans born between 1928 and 1945, just before the baby boomers. Technology might be suspected of making people more eager to position themselves in public than they would otherwise be, to judge from the fact that 20 percent of Millennials have posted videos of themselves online, in contrast with a modest 7 percent of the population as a whole.

An amazing—or frightening—81 percent of all Millennials have created their own website, and 59 percent of Millennials visit the social networking site they use most at least daily. A statistic that Pew doesn't share, but that is probably huge, is the number of Millennials who visit social networking websites several times a day. Cell phones, of course, have long been old hat to most Americans (even a majority of the Silents owns one), but 83 percent of Millennials place their cell phone next to their bedside when they sleep. Indeed, on an anecdotal basis, many Millennials appear to employ cell phones as their only telephone communication. In fact, 86 percent of Millennials use their cell phones to send or receive text messages. (A word of warning to drivers: 62 percent of Millennials admit to texting via cell phone while driving, a highly dangerous practice.) In short, according to the Pew study, Millennials have developed an entirely different system of social networking and for communicating their views on important issues with each other than was typical of all the still-living generations of Americans with whom they can be compared. Inevitably, this has affected the ways they relate to religious belief.

In the Pew Forum study, there is something to please many communities in the United States. Democratic pollsters and prognosticators, for example, might be rubbing their hands with glee over the finding that Millennials tend to describe themselves as liberal rather than conservative (29 percent to 28 percent), in contrast with older generations of Americans who tend to describe themselves as conservative. In the 2008 presidential election, according to Pew, Millennials who voted did so overwhelmingly for Barack Obama (66 percent).[2] But the rub may lie in the phrase "who voted." Many studies of political habits among different American generations have concluded that young people are significantly less likely to vote in national elections than their elders. Pew confirms this by finding that 69 percent of Millennials say they "always" or "almost always" vote, compared with Generation X (Americans born between 1965 and 1980) at 85 percent, baby boomers at 89 percent, and the Silents at 91 percent. In addition, Pew found that the "political enthusiasms of Millennials have cooled" since the 2008 election, with about half the Millennials telling Pew that President Obama had failed to change the way Washington worked, despite his campaign promises to do so.[3]

The liberal leaning of Millennials on social issues raised by the Pew Forum researchers shows up strongly in their attitudes toward single parenting and gay marriage. Some 54 percent of Millennials polled said that they had a close friend or a family member who was gay, and 63 percent said they thought that gay relationships ought to be accepted by society. By a striking margin of 50 percent to 36 percent, according to Pew, Millennials said they favored gay marriage. By contrast, 50 percent of the United States population as a whole is opposed to the concept of gay marriage, according to Pew, and in fact other polls have suggested that 62 percent of Americans support traditional marriage. Even on the question of attitudes toward gays, however, Millennials showed a striking change of heart between polling done on the issue in 2007 and polling done in 2010. In 2007, 47 percent of Millennials thought that gays raising children was just fine. By 2010, only 32 percent did. On the question of single women having children, however, Millennials strongly disapproved of the trend, with 69 percent against and 34 for it.[4]

The inclination of Millennials to favor government intervention in national affairs is demonstrated by a majority of 54 percent who said they thought the government was doing a good job of intervening in the economy, as opposed to 42 percent who said they thought the government was too involved in the ordering of national life. Other polls have shown that the Millennials are the first Americans in history to have a favorable attitude toward socialism.[5] On the other hand, and perhaps contradictorily, Millennials had a more favorable attitude toward business than older Americans. Some 44 percent of Millennials said they supported business, compared with 35 percent of Generation X and a measly 32 percent of the Silent Generation.

Where observers of American Christianity might sit up and take notice is where the Pew Forum study makes a major generalization about the apparent lack of religiosity of Millennials. Pew says flatly, "They are the least overtly religious generation in modern times. One-in-four are unaffiliated with any religion, far more than the share of other adults when they were ages 18 to 29."[6] In fact, of the approximately fifty million Americans who comprise the Millennials, one quarter is unaffiliated with any faith, and a further 10 percent consider themselves atheists or agnostics. Only 15 percent of Millennials say that living "a very religious life" is important to them, by contrast with 21 percent of those thirty and older. A far smaller percentage of unaffiliated, atheist, or agnostic people can be found in Americans who are in their thirties or forties.

Millennials attend church weekly in numbers slightly lower than people older than them (about 30 percent versus 41 percent for the general American population). The Pew Forum asserts that the intensity of belief among Millennials who claim to be Christians is as strong as it was among their elders at comparable periods of their lives, but some of the Pew figures, and significant research by others, suggests otherwise. For example, 77 percent of the general population say that they believe there are absolute moral standards, whereas Millennials who agree constitute 76 percent. Millennials told Pew researchers that they were much less convinced of God's existence than their elders, a rather unimpressive 64 percent compared with 73 percent of the generations above the age of thirty. When it comes to prayer habits, fewer than half (48 percent) of Millennials claim to pray every day, compared with 56 percent of Americans aged thirty to forty-nine, 61 percent of those in their fifties and early sixties, and 68 percent of those sixty-five and older.

As far as the Bible is concerned, 27 percent of Millennials believe that it is the literal Word of God, compared with 33 percent of the population as a whole. Despite this apparently greater skepticism toward the Bible, 74 percent of Millennials claim to believe in heaven. Hell is a less popular place to believe in, eliciting the faith of only 62 percent of Millennials. Analogous figures for the general population are similar: 74 percent of all Americans say they believe in heaven, but only 59 percent apparently believe in hell. Oddly, however, when it comes to the religiously affiliated among the Millennials, 29 percent say that only their own faith will lead to eternal life, whereas 66 percent of them believe that many religions can lead to eternal life. Counterintuitively, perhaps, only the Silents have a higher percentage of Americans who believe that other ways to eternal life may be as valid as those of their own faith.[7] Whereas 76 percent of the total American population described itself as Christian, the figure for Millennials was significantly lower: 68 percent.[8] The percentage of the general population of Americans who claim to be "absolutely certain about the existence of God" is 71 percent. Among Americans sixty-five or older—perhaps more conscious of approaching mortality than the rest—that figure is 77 percent, but only 64 percent of Millennials claim to have the same certainty in their minds about the existence of God.[9]

The lack of clarity about the idea of God's existence may account for the popularity among Millennials of the idea of evolution as offering the best explanation of life's origins. Some 55 percent of them embraced evolution as the best explanation for the origins of human life, compared with 48 percent of the total population and a much more modest 40 percent of Americans sixty-five and older.

Before moving on from the Pew study, I wish to highlight two intriguing findings about Millennials that do not quite fit the picture of a generation that is, according to Pew, "liberal, upbeat and open to change." Millennials are part of the two-thirds of Americans who feel that older people have better values than any younger generation. Pew asserts that most Americans believe that older people are superior to young people "when it comes to values and morals." By contrast, in the area of race relations, young people (i.e., the Millennials) are regarded by most Americans as more tolerant of races and groups different from their own than older Americans. Older Americans, according to Pew, agree with younger ones that young people's attitudes on race are more tolerant than that of earlier generations.[10]

Yet Millennials, believing as they apparently do in the superiority of evolution as an explanation of human origins, nevertheless agree overwhelmingly—and contradictorily—that there are absolute standards of right and wrong. Millennials score 76 percent in this area, almost identical with the percentage of the population as a whole.[11]

A number of writers have glanced at the Pew findings on Millennials, as well as other material on their generation, and thrown up their hands in despair. Robert Wuthnow, author of *After the Baby Boomers*, doesn't quite do this, but he comes close. "It may seem overly pessimistic," he writes, "to suggest that the future of American religion is in doubt just because religious leaders are not doing more to enlist the energies of younger adults."[12] But the "young adults," aka Millennials, are a quirky bunch. Naomi Schaefer Riley, in her interesting survey of some American faith-based colleges—she includes Mormon, Jewish, Catholic, and Protestant colleges in her book—makes the assertion that a UCLA survey of spirituality in higher education found that 75 percent of undergraduates were "searching for meaning or purpose in life."[13] According to the Pew study, however, Millennials are not so much searching for a single answer as picking and choosing in the supermarket of big ideas as they wander the aisles of the store with their shopping cart. Other studies, a few of which we will touch on, focus on the point that Millennials tend to have a supermarket approach toward religion.

NATIONAL STUDY ON YOUTH AND RELIGION

By far the most thorough and deep examination of teenagers in recent American history was the National Study on Youth and Religion, a research program directed by Christian Smith, professor in the department of sociology at the University of Notre Dame, and Lisa Pearce, assistant professor of sociology at the University of North Carolina at Chapel Hill. The project was supported financially by the Lilly Endowment and was conducted initially between August 2001 and 2003. An initial telephone survey of 3,290 people between thirteen and twenty-seven years old was followed up by 267 in-depth interviews with participants in 45 states. The initial results were published in Smith's book *Soul-Searching: The Religious and Spiritual Lives of American Teenagers*.[14] This was followed by a later volume, with Patricia Snell, called *Souls in Transition: The Religious and Spiritual Lives of Emerging Adults*.[15] Of course, the Smith and Snell studies spanned both a part of the Pew Millennials and part of Generation X. "The real point of religion, ultimately," a young person told the researcher-writer team Smith and Snell, "is to help people be good, to live good lives."[16]

Assuming for the moment that this perception is correct, that postmodern hiccup about the supposed relativity of all religious truth keeps coming back when the issue of the truth or falsehood of various religious claims crops up. "What do you mean by religious truth?" an interviewee asked Smith and Snell. "Because all religions pretty much have a good message that people can follow. I would say that the basic premise of the religions, like where they get their message from, is false, but the message itself is good."[17]

A more important point may be that Millennials, even if they regard all religions as more or less equally benign, are just not that interested in religion. They have too many other things to do. Between tweeting, texting each other, following Facebook entries, keeping up with Jon Stewart on Comedy Central, and going to college when they have nothing else to do, their lives are pretty packed. Their attention spans, already squeezed ever tighter by the relentless shortening of TV and video sound bites, may find it difficult to give the time of day to the entire subject of religion.

In fact, some observers may think going to college seems like a spare-time hobby for some Millennials, but a large number of them do it in order to acquire qualifications that they hope will get them well-paying jobs. Some 39 percent of Millennials are in college, graduate school, or trade school, and Pew estimates that more than half of Millennials will eventually have college degrees.[18]

The apparent competition for the time of these emerging young adults is likely to fragment attention significantly. This is indeed what some researchers on the attitudes of Millennials have discovered. Wuthnow writes, "The single word that best describes young adults' approach to religion and spirituality—indeed life—is tinkering. A tinkerer puts together a life from whatever skills, ideas, and resources that are readily at hand." Wuthnow uses the French word for tinkering—*bricolage*—and fleshes it out. "So it is with religion and spirituality," he writes. "We piece together our thoughts about religion and our interests in spirituality from the materials at hand. . . . *Bricolage* is thus an apt description of the religion and spirituality of young adults."[19]

A 2006 study of Millennials (though the term "Millennial" is not used; "twenty-somethings" is the rather clumsier synonym) by the Barna Group asserted that "twenty-somethings continue to be the most spiritually independent and resistant age group in America. Most of them pull away from participation and engagement in Christian churches, particularly during the college years. The research shows that, compared to older adults, twenty-somethings have significantly lower levels of church attendance, time spent alone studying and reading the Bible, volunteering to help churches, donations to churches, Sunday school and small group involvement, and use of Christian media (including television, radio, and magazines)."[20] Of course, baby boomers at the same age as Millennials of the past decade were similarly less interested in religion, but not, apparently, to the same degree.

Some 36 percent of twenty-somethings qualify as "born again Christians," according to Barna, and that is a lower figure than the 44 percent of those expressing the same faith values aged forty or more. The Barna survey, conducted over a relatively long period of time, January 2001 to August 2006, also revealed that the attitudes of the twenty-somethings had been affected by factors like the dramatic growth in higher education, the delayed onset of marriage, anticipation of sudden—and sometimes unwelcome—changes in their chosen careers, and willingness of parents to extend support well into the late twenties of their offspring. Young adults, said Barna, had therefore come into the expectation of an extended life transition.[21] Some of the young people might expect not to have dealt with the major life transitions of young adulthood until they are forty years old.

According to Barna, in fact, the most potent data regarding disengagement is that a majority of twenty-somethings—61 percent of today's young adults—had been churched at one point during their teen years but were now spiritually disengaged (i.e., not actively attending church, reading the Bible, or praying).

Only one-fifth of twenty-somethings, the report went on to say, had maintained a level of spiritual activity consistent with their high school experiences. Another one-fifth of teens were never significantly reached by a Christian community of faith during their teens and had also remained disconnected from the Christian faith.

For most adults, Barna said, this pattern of disengagement was "not merely a temporary phase in which they test the boundaries of independence, but is one that continues deeper into adulthood, with those in their thirties also less likely than older adults to be religiously active."[22]

David Kinnaman, the director of the Barna research for this report, made the following argument:

> There is considerable debate about whether the disengagement of twenty-somethings is a life stage issue—that is, a predictable element in the progression of people's development as they go through various family, occupational and chronological stages—or whether it is unique to this generation. While there is some truth to both explanations, this debate misses the point, which is that the current state of ministry to twenty-somethings is woefully inadequate to address the spiritual needs of millions of young adults. These individuals are making significant life choices and determining the patterns and preferences of their spiritual reality while churches wait, generally in vain, for them to return after college or when the kids come. When and if young adults do return to churches, it is difficult to convince them that a passionate pursuit of Christ is anything more than a nice add-on to their cluttered lifestyle.[23]

In other words, people who want to draw young people in America back to a Christian worldview and faith and from a worldview that is either hostile to, indifferent to, or at best mildly tolerant of religion need to understand precisely whom they are dealing with.

UNCHRISTIAN

Kinnaman's book *UnChristian: What a New Generation Really Thinks about Christianity . . . and Why It Matters*, coauthored by Gabe Lyons, reveals a devastatingly unattractive view of Christians and even Christianity among two categories of young people: both those brought up within the church but recently somewhat alienated and non-Christian groups (atheist, agnostic, followers of other faiths).[24] "Christianity," say the authors at the beginning of their book, "has an image problem."[25] "Our most recent data," they say later on in the book, "show that young outsiders have lost much of their respect for the Christian faith. These days nearly two out of every five young outsiders (38 percent) claim to have a 'bad impression of present-day Christianity.' . . . Outsiders direct their skepticism toward all things Christian: the faith itself, the people who profess it, the Bible, *and* Jesus Christ. . . . Young outsiders are most likely to be frustrated with present-day expressions of Christianity, followed by their aggravation with Christians."[26]

Christians, say Kinnaman and Lyons, "are primarily perceived for what they stand against. We have become famous for what we oppose, rather than who we are for. . . . In our national surveys with young people, we found the three most common perceptions of present-day Christianity are anti-homosexual (an image held by 91 percent of young outsiders), judgmental (87 percent), and hypocritical (85 percent)."[27] They add, "only a small percentage of outsiders strongly believe that the labels 'respect, love, hope, and trust' described Christianity."[28] Kinnaman and Lyons actually subdivided the young people they surveyed into Mosaics (born between 1984 and 2002) and Busters (born between 1965 and 1983). The opinions of Mosaics and Busters overlapped to a considerable extent.

Christian Smith's study, which contains detailed accounts of some of the 267 follow-up interviews the National Study on Youth and Religion (NSYR) undertook, was striking in its overall depiction of a "feel-good spirituality" expressed by the emerging adult interviewees. Smith describes a dominant theme of youth attitudes towards religion as "Therapeutic Moralistic Deism." This worldview holds that all religions in the world basically "share the same core principles, at least those that are important. All religions teach belief in God and the need to be a good person. These things are what really matters."[29]

The worldview behind this attitude holds the following things: First, there is a God who exists who created and orders the world and watches over human life on earth. Second, to quote Smith's book specifically, "God wants people to be good, nice, and fair to each other, as taught in the Bible and by most world religions. Third, the central goal of life is to be happy and to feel good about oneself. Fourth, God does not need to be particularly involved in one's life except when God is needed to resolve a problem. Fifth, good people go to heaven when they die."[30] Under the umbrella of this "feel-good spirituality," says Smith, three quarters of the emerging adults claim to be Christians, but only one half of those consider this to be a matter of importance.

According to Smith and Snell and other writers, to unpack Therapeutic Moral Deism is to discover a huge emphasis on feeling as the basic determinant of right and wrong, a view that God is only mildly concerned with the human race and exists primarily to respond to emergency calls, and a belief that all religions are more or less the same.

What Smith uncovered was not simply a skittishness about conviction but a striking lack of belief in a shared reality of life that applies to all people: a view of the universe where there are no agreed-upon ways of reasoning through different choices. Smith writes, "Whether or not they use these words to say it, for most emerging adults, it's all relative. One thought or opinion isn't more defensible than another. One way of life cannot claim to be better than others. Some moral beliefs may personally feel right, but no moral belief can rationally claim to be really true."[31]

Smith and others have noted that the phrase "I feel that" has almost ubiquitously replaced the phrases "I think that," "I believe that," and "I would argue that"—"a shift in language use that express[es] an essentially subjectivistic and emotivistic approach to moral reasoning and rational argument . . . which leads to speech in which claims are not staked, rational arguments are not developed, differences are not engaged, nature is not referenced, and universals are not recognized. Rather, differences in viewpoints and ways of life are mostly acknowledged, respected, and then set aside as incommensurate and off limits for evaluation."[32]

As Smith discovered in his research, the young adults researchers spoke with often reverted in conversation to a highly personalized, subjective form of discourse characteristic of the postmodern world where they are—their parents surely hope—grappling with real life and growing into maturity. Today's emerging adults, the authors write, have become trapped in a postmodern culture that stresses "difference over unity, relativity over universals, subjective experience over rational authorities, feeling over reason." In this cultural environment, Smith and Snell write, there is little reason to be hostile toward organized religion, but there is also little reason to pursue it either.[33]

Since there is no agreed-upon standard of truth and reality, today's emerging adults pick and choose the way they behave on the basis of whatever subjective impression of life they may have recently encountered. There is no concept of an objective morality. It is all a question of response to feeling, Smith and Snell report; if it feels wrong, it is wrong. Most emerging adults would say, "If something hurts another person, it is probably bad; if it does not and is not illegal, it's probably fine." They conclude, "It was clear in many interviews that emerging adults felt entirely comfortable describing various religious beliefs that they affirmed but that appeared to have no connection to any religious moral teaching from their teen years." "The vast majority of emerging adults nonetheless believe," Smith and Snell write, "that cohabiting is a smart if not absolutely necessary experience and phase for moving toward an eventual successful and happy marriage. . . . None of the emerging adults who are enthusiastic about cohabiting as a means to prevent unsuccessful marriages seem aware that nearly all studies consistently show that couples who live together before their weddings are more, not less, likely to later divorce than [conventionally chaste] couples."[34]

The bland relativistic assumptions of such attitudes surprised some of the NSYR researchers. The authors write, "Whether or not they use these words to say it, for most emerging adults, it's all relative. . . . One way of life cannot claim to be better than others."[35] Smith concedes that "such a condition arguably encourages the true virtues of humility and openness to difference—precious commodities, we think, that are all too scarce in the world today." He qualifies that comment, however, with the comment, "But when life's push comes to shove for emerging adults, such a condition also thwarts many of them from ever being able to decide what they believe is really true, right, and good."[36]

Princeton Theological Seminary Professor and youth minister Kenda Creasy Dean wrote up her own troubling conclusions in the book *Almost Christian: What the Faith of Our Teenagers Is Telling the American Church*.[37] Dean thinks that the religious concoction written about by Smith, Therapeutic Moralistic Deism, is an "imposter faith" that is nevertheless supplanting Christianity as the dominant religion in American churches.[38] The "imposter faith," Dean says, poses as Christianity but "in fact lacks the holy desire and fissional clarity necessary for Christian discipleship." American teenagers, Dean says, have unwittingly been feeding on "a bargain religion, cheap but unsatisfying, whose gods require little in the way of fidelity of sacrifice."[39]

Dean came up with the title of her book *Almost Christian* from the fact that during the Great Awakening in eighteenth-century England, the evangelists George Whitefield and John Wesley both preached sermons on the difference between an "almost Christian" and an "altogether Christian." (The phrase is derived from the incident in Acts 26:28 when King Agrippa says to the apostle Paul, "Almost thou persuadest me to be a Christian.") Dean explains,

> For Wesley, the difference between an "almost Christian" and an "altogether Christian" boiled down to love: [quoting Wesley] "The great question of all, then, still remains. Is the

> love of God shed abroad in your heart? Can you cry out, 'My God, and my All'? Do you desire nothing but him? Are you happy in God? Is he your glory, your delight, your crown of rejoicing? Is this commandment written in your heart, 'That he who loveth God love his brother also'? Do you then love your neighbor as yourself? Do you love every man, even your enemies, even the enemies of God as your own should? As Christ loved you?"[40]

Dean suggests that Therapeutic Moralistic Deism among teenagers and American young people is actually adults' fault. She says, "Since the religious and spiritual choices of American teenagers echo, with astonishing clarity, the religious and spiritual choice of the adults who love them, lackadaisical faith is not young people's issue, but ours." In short, rather than blaming young people for their toothless, feel-good, ersatz Christianity, it is the adults who have committed themselves to nurturing the next generation of Christian believers who are to blame.[41] Smith takes this one step further: the religion of Therapeutic Moralistic Deism is actually an expression of the triumph of liberal Protestantism in the larger American culture.

"Liberal Protestants," says sociologist N. Jay Demerath, "have lost structurally at the micro level precisely because they won culturally at the macro level."[42] Smith makes the case that the core values of liberal Protestantism—"individualism, pluralism, emancipation, tolerance, free critical inquiry, and the authority of human experience"—have come to "permeate broader American culture."[43] In fact, statistics show, half of all pastors would leave the ministry tomorrow if they could. Seventy percent are fighting depression, and 90 percent can't cope with the challenges of ministry.[44]

Many adults, Smith asserts, despite belonging in some cases to evangelical churches, are comfortable with the liberal faith described sardonically in 1937 by Yale University theologian H. Richard Niebuhr. This liberal theology holds that "a God without wrath brought men without sin into a kingdom without judgment through the ministrations of a Christ without a cross."[45] In short, even though evangelical Christian churches in the United States are gaining membership numbers far more rapidly than churches with a liberal theology, in Smith's view the National Study on Youth and Religion may have demonstrated a worrying feature of Christianity in contemporary American culture: evangelical Christians have won the battle for church membership, but they may have lost the larger cultural war.

There are, of course, as we shall see in chapter 5, signs that American young people, in different parts of the country, are again coming alive in their Christian faith. It is becoming increasingly obvious, however, that none of the comfortable assumptions about the influence on society of America's "civic religion," a sort of Christianity lite, can be maintained. By the 1950s, the post-war neo-evangelical movement largely identified with the crusades of Billy Graham had succumbed in some respects to its own success. It didn't really threaten any American community other than hard-core atheists. But in becoming a complacent civic religion, Christianity in America seemed to have lost its bite, its tenacious presence at the heart of the American experiment in freedom and self-government.

This raises an issue that is as controversial as Christianity has always been: Was America ever really Christian? If so, in what way? If it no longer is, as Jon Meacham's cover story in *Newsweek* contended, how did the erosion of what had been an American Christian core take place?

The steady progress of secularism in transforming the culture and in affecting the ways people think about the Christian faith is the topic of chapter 4. It's a revealing story. But first we must look at what the powerful engine of freedom, prosperity, and social virtue American Christianity was for at least the first two and a half centuries of the nation's existence.

3

Was America Ever a Christian Nation?

The Intention to Form a Christian Community

Was America ever Christian? Did its inhabitants—most of them, at any rate—at one time constitute a community of Christian believers? Since its formation as a nation, of course, America has chosen not to be officially identified with any actual religion. The First Amendment as it relates to religion is as well known to opponents of the Christian presence in American public life as to its defenders: "Congress shall make no law respecting an establishment of religion, or prohibiting the free exercise thereof." Even the laziest attendee of a sixth-grade civics class knows that the founders did not want any religious organization or denomination to enjoy a government-conferred advantage in the competition for followers. After all, as we shall see, many supporters of the American Revolution defined their struggle for independence from Great Britain as much in religious terms as in purely political terms.

Still, the key question remains: Was America ever a Christian country in the same sense that we can say, for example, Algeria is a Muslim country? The answer to that question is much less complicated than it might seem to some. If, let's say, about 90 percent or more of the population thought of themselves as Christian, even if they never actually set foot in a church, would it be unreasonable to say that the population was overwhelmingly Christian? I think it would be very reasonable to think that, in the same sense that Algeria is a Muslim country, America at one point was Christian.

You will, of course, find a multitude of American college professors who would not agree with that position. It irks many American intellectuals who have adopted a predominantly secular worldview that the overwhelming majority of Americans through most of American history up until the second half of the twentieth century didn't share their secularist position. Actually, it has been the aggressive assault on America's Christian beginnings in public debate over the past few decades that has led many conservative Christians to long for a return to a more traditional America—an America that they certainly assume was more "Christian."

For example, from the 1970s on, quite a few new books were published that said, yes, America *was* once Christian. Such books expressed a longing among many conservative Americans for a return to a time when America was relatively untouched by the cult of sexual gratification, the drug culture, and the rejection of most values that had usually been considered "traditional." The 1960s were a time of immense turbulence in

American national life, not just because of anti–Vietnam War protests that roiled much of the country but also because of a conscious youth rebellion against moral restraints on personal behavior that Americans had in general respected as normative, even if they hadn't always been able to observe them. When the first backlash against the 1960s American cultural revolution began a decade later, the American Christian conservative movement, later identified with such personalities as Rev. Jerry Falwell and Rev. Pat Robertson, began to coalesce around the idea that America had once been "Christian" but had sort of lost its virtue in the upheavals of the 1960s. Ardent secularists probably derided such an idea as a sheer myth, but if it was ever a myth, it was a powerful one that was as reassuring as it was attractive.

Several books appeared that argued that America had actually been providentially brought into existence specifically to be a "Christian" nation—a nation with a prophetic destiny to bless, if possible, the rest of the world. The authors of these books suggested that recently America had lost its way not simply by failing to maintain the godly values espoused by most of the first English settlers to live on the American continent but by losing sight of America's purpose to be a "godly" nation.

PROVIDENTIALISM

Of the many books that set off to try to prove that America had been founded as a Christian covenant community in a providential plan devised by the Almighty himself, few had more popularity and influence among American evangelical Christians than *The Light and the Glory* by Peter Marshall and David Manuel. First published in 1977 by a Christian publishing house,

Fleming H. Revell, the book sold (in hardcover and softcover versions) more than six hundred thousand copies. It was a gigantic bestseller and may well have been read by hundreds of thousands of other readers who never actually purchased a copy. Nine years later Marshall and Manuel followed up with another book continuing the story of America from the perspective of possible—indeed probable—Christian providence, *From Sea to Shining Sea*. As recently as 2009, a new version of *The Light and the Glory* appeared.[1]

The Light and the Glory actually begins its tale through the eyes of Christopher Columbus who, the authors claimed, had expressed the belief that his discovery of the New World had been a divinely originated call upon his life. Marshall and Manuel's theme is unabashedly simple: just as the ancient Israelites in the Old Testament story sensed a corporate call of God upon their nation, so the inhabitants of America, from the Pilgrim Fathers onward, had inherited a corporate relationship with God that required them to behave in a godly way and, when necessary, to bow their heads in national repentance. Writ large, this is the core of the idea of "American exceptionalism."

The two authors acknowledged that many Christians in the modern era believed that the idea of corporate communities having a covenantal relationship with God had been eliminated once Jesus Christ appeared. The Old Testament Israelites, such Christian thinkers and theologians argued, had functioned as a community led by Jehovah, the almighty God, during the period when Israel was being formed as a nation and being led out of Egypt into the Promised Land. After the coming of Christ, according to Marshall and Manuel, many Christians believed that no ethnic or national community in the world could maintain a *corporate* relationship with God. That possibility surely had come to an end once the New Testament had come into existence. "But what if," Marshall and Manuel asked, "in particular, [God] had a plan for those He would bring to America, a plan which saw this continent as the stage for a new act in the drama of mankind's redemption? Could it be that we Americans, as a people, were meant to be a 'light to lighten the Gentiles' (Luke 2:32)—a demonstration to the world of how God intended his children to live together under the Lordship of Christ? Was our vast divergence from this blueprint," the authors asked, "after such a promising beginning, the reason why we now seem to be heading into a new dark age?"[2]

The Light and the Glory belongs to the category of historical interpretation that is sometimes called "providentialism," the notion that certain events in history are guided by a divine hand in a providential way for the benefit of the participants or their successors and others, albeit for God's ultimate purposes. It is, of course, a way of understanding our past that is comforting and reassuring. It implies that there was a sort of providential blueprint for America from its first days of European, and particularly English, settlement. It is fair to say that until the twentieth century, American historical writing and even American legal writing, at both the academic and the popular level, was deeply influenced by a self-conscious providentialism. Even such secular concepts as "manifest destiny," the American belief that America was providentially destined, even duty-bound, to extend its political and cultural power ever-further westward (not stopping, according to some interpreters, on the West Coast of the American continent but leaping across the Pacific to the lands there) derived much of its force from Christian providentialism.

This perspective is very popular among Christian conservatives, for it reinforces their conviction that their perspectives on national and international policy are natural heirs to the ideas shared by the first English colonial settlers in North America and later articulated in the concepts that led to the American Revolution. Indeed, it is almost an axiom of American Christian "providentialists" that the nation was founded with the explicit intention of embodying and advancing the ideas of Christian nationhood. It's interesting that George Washington himself, in his first inaugural address, said, "No people can be bound to acknowledge and adore the Invisible Hand which conducts the affairs of men more than the people of the United States."[3] John Adams, our second president, after he had left office, wrote on July 4, 1821, "The highest, the transcendent glory of the American Revolution was this—it connected, in one indissoluble bond, the principles of civil government with the precepts of Christianity."[4]

Agnostics and atheists, of course, pooh-pooh this whole idea. Since the whole of creation, and therefore the whole of history, is a series of accidents, they argue, there is no such entity as Providence guiding anything. Richard Dawkins is quoted as saying, "The universe we observe has precisely the properties we should expect if there is, at bottom, no design, no purpose, no evil and no good, nothing but blind, pitiless indifference."[5]

According to Dawkins and most atheists who based their view on the supposed discoveries of science, life is simply this: a random series of purposeless events with no guiding hand whatsoever. Marxists, of course, believe that all of history is unraveling according to the economic imperatives of inexorable economic and sociological laws. For them, "destiny" is fulfilled when Marxists gain the levers of political power and manipulate life on earth until every man, woman, and child at some undetermined point in the future will find themselves living in the utopian paradise of Communism. At that point, Marxists believe, there will be no war, no crime, no serious social problems because rational economic developments will have rendered them all irrelevant.

But it is not just the Marxists and other unbelievers who are quite hostile to the notion of providential history. A significant and perhaps growing portion of respected Christian historians and thinkers completely reject the idea that America ever was distinctly Christian. Such thinkers and writers, indeed, completely reject the possibility that the American Revolution was a divinely inspired and divinely guided series of events whose purpose was to advance the cause of Christianity in one particular part of the world, namely the new nation that became the United States. More than two decades ago, evangelical historians Mark Noll, Nathan Hatch, and George Marsden collaborated on a book that said it sought "to examine carefully the popular belief that America was once a 'Christian nation' which has now been all but overrun by secular humanism. To put it most simply: is this a factual picture, a mythical picture, or something else altogether?"

The authors stated their conclusion early on in the book. It was their opinion that "early American history does not deserve to be considered uniquely, distinctly or even predominantly Christian, if we mean by the word 'Christian' a state of society reflecting the ideals presented in Scripture. There is no lost golden age to which American Christians may return." The trio also concluded that "careful examination of Christian teaching on government, the state, and the nature of culture shows that the idea of a 'Christian nation' is a very ambiguous concept which is usually harmful to effective Christian action in society."[6]

CHRISTIAN NATIONALISM

This overall skeptical view of the Christian providentialist interpretation of American history is shared by John Fea, author of the much more recent volume *Was America Founded as a Christian Nation?*[7] Fea writes negatively of what he calls "Christian nationalism"—a view of history that interprets most of what happened in America since the first colonial settlements as demonstrating the finger of God. He partly shows his hand by complaining that "the Christian Right," a term that usually carries a derogatory connotation, habitually "use[es] Washington's supposed Christianity to help promote their cultural agenda for contemporary America."[8] Fea fails to define either "the Christian Right" or what its "cultural agenda" might be. (If he means Christian conservatives, then there is wide breadth of difference among them on a cultural agenda for the contemporary United States.) The core of his argument, which is essentially shared by Noll, Hatch, and Marsden, is as follows:

1. There is "little evidence to suggest that Christianity permeated the culture and value system of the colony,"[9] and even if there were strong communities of Christians here and there, the society in which they lived in New England was too flawed to deserve the term "Christian."
2. The English colonists of the sixteenth and seventeenth centuries couldn't have been serious Christians because almost all of them accepted slavery as a fact of life. Also—and this is certainly true historically—the Puritan Christians who established large and powerful communities in New England were, by today's standards, sometimes harshly intolerant of religious diversity.
3. The most important founders of America in the Revolutionary period were not really Christians but an eclectic

gathering of eighteenth-century intellectuals who may have shared views in common on the importance of Christian ethical behavior as defined in their day but were at variance with each other theologically, from Unitarian to Deist, and thus could not really have agreed on any notion of how America might become, let alone actually be, "Christian."

4. Church attendance in the colonies at the time of the Revolution was probably no more than 15 percent of the population, thus demonstrating that it was politics more than spiritual concerns that motivated the Revolution.

The two main issues mentioned in this critique need to be separated from each other. First, how serious were most of the colonial settlers of the seventeenth century about establishing a Christian community in the New World? Second, at the time of the Revolution and shortly thereafter, how prominent were the views of evangelical Christians?

The story of the first English settlers in North America has been frequently and elaborately told in many accounts of early American history. Broadly speaking, there is a consensus that the first permanent English settlement in North America, the one at Jamestown in Virginia, was inspired by different motives from those held by the Puritans in the New England settlement. Christopher Newport captained the *Susan Constant*, the largest of three ships—along with the *Godspeed* and the *Discovery*—that made landfall at Cape Henry in Virginia on April 26, 1607. The Virginia Company that was formed in London in 1606 had been granted a charter by King James I of England, who insisted that the purpose of the company was "propagating all Christian religions to such people as yet live in darkness and miserable ignorance of the true knowledge and worship of God."[10]

But John Smith, the man who became leader of the colonists on the written instructions of the Virginia Company, was genuinely skeptical about any religious motive in the initial settlement of Virginia. "For, I am not so simple to think that ever any other motive than wealth will erect there a commonwealth," he wrote on his return to England in 1609. In fact, he mocked the pretensions of company publicists that piety was involved at all in the exploration of North America via Virginia. Those propagandists for settlement, he averred, were "making religion their colour when all their aime was nothing but present profit."[11]

The Jamestown settlement nearly went extinct during the "starving time" of 1608–1610, but after the handful of surviving colonists were rescued by the timely arrival of a well-provisioned fleet under the command of Lord De La Marr, a new order of discipline was imposed. After his arrival in 1610, De La Marr's first action was to convene a church service in which the colonists would be called to sacrifice and industry. There was then a steady influx of new colonists.

By 1619 the number of settlers, all single men, was around two thousand. That year was marked by three landmark events in the colony's history. The first was the arrival of a ship from England with ninety "young maidens" (to the great delight of the colonists) who offered themselves in marriage to any colonist who could afford the cost of her trip across the Atlantic. The second historic event was the landing of twenty African chattel slaves from a Dutch trading ship. This marked the sad beginning of the African slave trade with Virginia and other states further south. The third was the convening in the Jamestown church of a legislative assembly, the first ever in North America.

Despite the overtly money-seeking motivations of the first Virginia settlers, the majority of whom were indentured servants, the regime imposed by De La Marr introduced a legal code that made church attendance compulsory. John Rolfe, the colonist who married the Indian princess Pocahontas (credited with saving the life of John Smith) after she had been baptized as a Christian and renamed Rebecca, had introduced a new strain of tobacco that was much more popular with both the colonists and the infant tobacco market in England. But Rolfe gave evidence of being a man of more than simply mercenary interests. In a 1614 letter to Sir Thomas Dale, governor of Jamestown, Rolfe explained his marriage to Pocahontas, defending himself from cynical criticism that he was drawn to Pocahontas by nothing but carnal needs. He was, he wrote to Dale, "well assured in [his] perswasion (by the often triall and proving of my self, in my holiest meditations and praiers), that [he] had been called [into the marriage] by the spirit of God."[12] Rolfe thought of the settlers in distinct Old Testament Hebraic terms as a "chosen people." They were, he said, "a peculiar people, marked and chosen by the finger of God."

The Jamestown colonists were to experience greater trials in the future, notably a devastating massacre by Native Americans in 1622, yet for many years the recruitment of settlers in England included trolling the city streets for orphans, the desperately poor, and others who could satisfy the labor demands of the Virginia tobacco industry. As a company announcement said at one point, "The Citie of London have, by act of their common counsel, appointed One Hundred Children out of their superfluous multitudes to be transported to Virginia; there to be bound apprentices for certain years, and afterward with very beneficiall conditions for the Children. . . ." The same announcement made it clear that "it falleth out that among those Children, sundry being ill-disposed and fitter for any remote place than this City, declared their unwillingness to go to Virginia; of whom the City is especially desirous to be disburdened; and in Virginia under severe Masters they may be brought to goodness."[13]

Meanwhile, a group of pious separatists, Protestant Christians who wanted to be "disburdened" from the Church of England and its royal head, King Charles I, had migrated from the town of Scrooby in Nottinghamshire to Leiden, in the Netherlands. There they were welcomed and encouraged to practice their religion in any form they liked. For the first few years the voluntary exile had worked satisfactorily, but by 1620 they were anxious to move on. Their children were becoming "de-Englished," and their aspirations were to build a completely new society somewhere else. These were the original Pilgrim Fathers, a resolute, courageous group of Christians willing to face overwhelming odds to fulfill what they thought was a divine calling. They secured a patent from a London company to settle in America and secured a ship from England, the *Mayflower*, to transport them first to Plymouth, in the south of England, and then across the Atlantic.

They set sail from Plymouth, England, at a very inauspicious time, December 11, 1620, the beginning of one of the roughest weather seasons in the North Atlantic. Despite the stormy passage and the cramped accommodations, 102 men, women, and children crammed into a narrow space below deck and sailed forth into the North Atlantic. The passenger area was so crowded that no one had more space than a single bed, and the ceiling was so low that no one taller than five feet could stand up straight. All but two of the passengers and crew survived the journey. Of the two deaths, one was that of a sailor who had cruelly mocked the passengers with profane curses. He died the same day he contracted a mysterious fever that didn't afflict any of the other passengers or crew. The second death was of a Pilgrim who disobeyed instructions to maintain a daily consumption of lemon juice and who, as a consequence, died of scurvy.

The Mayflower had originally been intended to land its passengers at the mouth of the Hudson River under the patent granted to the London Virginia Company. However, when it approached land off Cape Cod, Massachusetts, the Pilgrim leaders were told by the captain that to continue the journey south to the Hudson would require lengthy and perhaps risky sailing. The leaders of the Pilgrims accordingly decided to disembark near where they had first sighted land, at what was to become Plymouth, Massachusetts. Without the authority from the London company to establish their colony there, however, the leaders proposed that the passengers on the ship sign a voluntary compact of self-government, the first such document in American history. Accordingly, all forty-one of the adult male passengers signed what has become known as the "Mayflower Compact," committing themselves to combine together into a "civil body politic." The Compact is surprisingly simple and hardly comprises a full-blooded political constitution, yet it makes clear that uppermost in the minds of the Pilgrim settlers in New England was (1) the spreading of Christianity, and (2) a covenant to act toward each other in mutual respect and submission. The Compact begins with an obligatory display of loyalty to King James of England and then proceeds to spell out what is being agreed upon. It reads:

> In the name of God, Amen. We whose names are underwritten, the loyal subjects of our dread Sovereign Lord King James, by the grace of God, of Great Britain, France, and

> Ireland, King, defender of the Faith etc. Having undertaken, for the Glory of God, and advancements of the Christian faith and honor of our King and Country, a voyage to plant the first colony in the Northern parts of Virginia, do by these presents, solemnly and mutually, in the presence of God and one another, covenant and combine ourselves together into a civil body politic; for our better ordering, and preservation and furtherance of the ends aforesaid; and by virtue hereof to enact, constitute, and frame, such just and equal laws, ordinances, acts, constitution, and offices, from time to time, as shall be through most meet and convenient for the general good of the colony; unto which we promise all due submission and obedience.
>
> In witness whereof we hereunto subscribed our names at Cape Cod the 11 of November, in the years of the reign of our Sovereign Lord King James, of England, France, and Ireland, the eighteenth, and of Scotland the fifty fourth, 1620.[14]

One of the signatories of the Compact was William Bradford, later to become the governor of Plymouth Colony and the first great eyewitness chronicler of the Pilgrims and of Plymouth. As he notes sadly in his account of the Pilgrims, *Of Plymouth Plantation*, more than half of the original Pilgrims who set foot in the New World in the winter of 1620 had died before the winter was over from hunger, exposure, and the ever-present scurvy that the lack of fresh fruit and vegetables in the diet brought on.[15] It was the heroic efforts of Bradford, Elder William Brewster, and the one experienced soldier in the group, Captain Miles Standish, that made possible the survival of the others. Yet by 1630, despite the replenishment of Plymouth's numbers by new arrivals, the population of the colony amounted to only about three hundred. Bradford wrote poignantly, "Thus out of small beginnings, greater things have been produced by

His hand that made all things of nothing, and gives being to all things that are; and as one small candle may light a thousands, so the light her kindled hath shone to many, yea in some sort to our whole nation; let the glorious name of Jehova have all the praise."[16]

The "one small candle" that Bradford was referring to had already set in motion the beginning of what became known as the Great Migration, a steady stream of Puritans from England seeking somewhere to live out their faith and their lives unencumbered by the Church of England or the increasingly anti-Puritan government of King Charles I. These Puritans were not separatists, as the Pilgrims had been: they were not repudiating the Church of England. They sought, however, to build a civil society much more reflective of their Christian values than would have been possible in England.

The man who epitomizes this facet of the Great Migration was John Winthrop. He was a successful London lawyer and landowner in the east of England. He was a leading figure in the founding of the Massachusetts Bay Company in 1629, obtaining a charter from the king that authorized the company to govern the colony it was about to form without having to refer back to anyone in London. King Charles had become increasingly intolerant towards Protestant nonconformists like the Puritans, and in March of 1629 he dissolved Parliament, beginning an eleven-year period of royal rule in England without Parliament. In October 1629, while still in England, Winthrop was elected governor of the Massachusetts Bay Colony and, increasingly worried by the development of events in England, began to gather supplies and recruit men with skills needed in the new community. The principal members of the Massachusetts Bay Company were Puritans, and they decided to take the entire company, with the rules of self-government approved by the king, to New England with them.

In April 1630, Winthrop was a passenger aboard the *Arbella*, one of four ships carrying four hundred migrants that assembled for sailing off the Isle of Wight on the south coast of England. During the voyage across the Atlantic aboard the *Arbella*, Winthrop delivered a sermon that has echoed throughout American history as an expression of the way American Christians—and then just Americans in general—have traditionally seen themselves: a special people with special responsibilities and, above all, generous toward each other and outsiders. The sermon was titled "A Model of Christian Charity," and the most frequently cited phrase from it has been, "For we must consider that we shall be as a city upon a hill. The eyes of all people are upon us."

In the twentieth century, at least two American presidents, John F. Kennedy and Ronald Reagan, cited the phrase as an affirmation that the United States as a nation has a unique responsibility to be a blessing to the world. Reagan, in fact, cited Winthrop's phrase, which is taken from the words of Jesus in the Sermon on the Mount (see Matt. 5:14), in his 1974 address to the Conservative Political Action Committee, but his better-known usage was in his farewell address as president in January 1989. He said, "I've spoken of the shining city all my political life, but I don't know if I ever quite communicated what I saw when I said it. But in my mind it was a tall, proud city built on rocks stronger than the oceans, wind-swept, God-blessed, and teeming with people of all kinds living in harmony and peace, a city with free ports that hummed with commerce and creativity, and if there had to be city walls, the walls had doors and the doors were open to anyone with the will and the heart to get there. That's how I saw it and see it still."[17]

But when people cite the "city on a hill" portion from Winthrop's speech, they usually fail to mention the rest of it, which is emphatic about three points. First, the Puritans setting off for the New World considered themselves bound together in a mutual covenant that had been freely entered into in God's presence. Second, they, and Winthrop, felt that God would keep faith with the Puritans if they kept faith with him, and third, God would "break out in wrath" against the community if it became worldly rather than godly. Winthrop preached,

> We are entered into covenant with Him for this work. We have taken out a commission. The Lord hath given us leave to draw our own articles. We have professed to enterprise these and those accounts, upon these and those ends. We have hereupon besought Him of favor and blessing. Now if the Lord shall please to hear us, and bring us in peace to the place we desire, then hath He ratified this covenant and sealed our commission, and will expect a strict performance of the articles contained in it; but if we shall neglect the observation of these articles which are the ends we have propounded, and, dissembling with our God, shall fall to embrace this present world and prosecute our carnal intentions, seeking great things for ourselves and our posterity, the Lord will surely break out in wrath against us, and be revenged of such a people, and make us know the price of the breach of such a covenant.[18]

What might be the consequences of disobedience against God's order? Winthrop answered the question, "But if our hearts shall turn away, so that we will not obey, but shall be seduced, and worship other Gods, our pleasure and profits, and serve them; it is propounded unto us this day, we shall surely perish out of the good land whither we pass over this vast sea to possess it." It was a classic Calvinist statement of man's fallenness and God's grace. The Puritans were Calvinists, and they believed that human beings were totally depraved and worthy of God's divine judgment. But they also believed that God, in his mercy, had selected those he would draw to himself before the foundation of the world. Nothing men or women could do would affect God's choice of who had been predestined for grace and salvation.

What therefore, Winthrop rhetorically asked, should be the principle of behavior to be demonstrated toward each other? Brotherly love. "That which most in their churches maintain as truth in profession only," Winthrop continues, "we must bring into familiar and constant practice; as in this duty of love, we must love brotherly without dissimulation, we must love one another with a pure heart fervently. We must bear one another's burdens. We must not look only on our own things, but also on the things of our brethren." The "love" of which Winthrop speaks is, he says, "like we shall find in the histories of the church, in all ages; the sweet sympathy of affections which was in the members of this body one towards another; their cheerfulness in serving and suffering together; how liberal they were without repining, harborers without grudging, and helpful without reproaching; and all from hence, because they had fervent love amongst them; which only makes the practice of mercy constant and easy."[19]

Because it has been fashionable since the twentieth century for many people to scorn the Puritans as repressive and intolerant, it is worth citing Winthrop's sermon at length to grasp how self-critical the Puritans were and how they held themselves to very high standards of behavior toward others. Indeed, it is probably reasonable to say that the Puritans, among America's founders, were more conscious of their human failings than almost any generation of Americans who professed the Christian faith.

They were also conscious that they were exceptional people, not in the sense of being superior to others but in the sense of being called by God to a unique purpose, quite similar to the Israelites on their journey from Egypt to Zion. They often referred to themselves as "the New Israel" and consciously sought to build a society much closer to Jewish society under the Mosaic Law. Winthrop, in fact, sought to build not only a model church but also a model state, legislating laws directly modeled on the Old Testament Torah. Indeed, in the early years there was capital punishment for offenses requiring such a punishment in the Old Testament: worshiping any god besides Jehovah, witchcraft, adultery, sodomy, and kidnapping. It was certainly not a society compatible with modern concepts of almost unrestrained self-indulgence.

The Sabbath was rigidly enforced, with citizens being prohibited even in their own homes from engaging in any activity that might be deemed work, and the civil and ecclesiastical society that Winthrop and his like-minded associates formed enjoyed a system of government that was far more open to broad political participation than in virtually any contemporary community in the Western world. Winthrop began governing the assembly of settlers, with seven "assistants," in August 1630. In October of 1630, an assembly of "the whole body of the settlers" decided that the "freemen of the colony," who were all in Massachusetts already, and not the stockholders of the company, should have the power of selecting "assistants" by choice, and selecting from among themselves the governor and the deputy governor. The assistants would in effect form a legislative body that would make laws for the colony. The clergy were strictly prohibited from participating in government.

The late historian Sydney Ahlstrom observed, "The Bay Colony governed itself by the resultant bicameral system without essential modification for over sixty years. To call it a 'theocracy' is therefore absurd. Its franchise was wider than England's, and of all the government in the Western world at the time, that of early Massachusetts gave the clergy least authority."[20] It was certainly a community that sought to embody what it believed were the set of civil laws closest to what the members thought most pleasing to God for the governance of any civil community, yet it clearly did not embrace the idea that pastors or other church leaders were inherently more qualified to assume governing power than ordinary laypeople.

Attractive as many features of the Massachusetts Bay Colony were, it was certainly no untroubled Christian utopia. There were frequent wars with the Indians—nowadays called Native Americans—who quickly discovered that the colonists had imported notions of land ownership derived from European practice and not at all from North America, where land usage (for hunting or agriculture) was far more important than legal title, a concept that was initially quite alien to the Indian tribes. Native Americans themselves, when they were even noticed, were often referred to condescendingly as "children" or, worse, as Canaanites whom the Puritans—the New Israel—had as much right to displace as the ancient Israelites had the right to displace the original inhabitants of the land of Canaan after the exodus from Egypt.

In fact, one of the first serious political controversies in the Bay Colony was with a brilliant, pious Puritan, Roger Williams, who made it a habit to behave as fairly as possible toward the

Indians. Williams offended the leadership of the colony when he insisted that church and state should be entirely separate from each other. Winthrop and Williams liked each other, although their opinions on numerous topics varied widely. Winthrop believed that God had created a covenant with an entire people, the New England settlers. Williams believed that God created covenants only with individual human beings. There should, he thought, be orderly secular rule in society, but the secular authorities had no right at all to interfere with a private individual's conscience. Williams, moreover, in his Christian theology, essentially believed that the individual conscience was the sole entity entitled to make religious judgments.

To the leadership of the Bay Colony, this was antinomianism, the view that Christians, because they attained righteousness by faith rather than through observance of the law, were not subject to moral laws upheld by any community. It was a dangerous heresy, because it seemed to invite those who upheld its principles to dissent from the behavioral norms of the community. Williams, moreover, seemed in some ways to be what contemporary people call a secularist, since he wanted to banish religion altogether from government. The Puritan settlers believed that no amount of good works could affect a believer's salvation. God had already decided that question in relation to everyone. But they also believed that there was a covenantal relationship between God and the community. This required the community to craft laws aligned as much as possible with biblical models, which in practice meant Old Testament laws. It also meant that preachers had to be careful to walk a narrow line between asserting the unconditional nature of God's grace toward individual believers and urging their congregations to hew to community laws and standards that they felt affirmed the community's covenant relationship with God. The tension between these two positions was to surface forcefully during the case involving Anne Hutchinson.

Winthrop had been deposed from the governorship in 1634 when the freemen of the colony found that the Massachusetts Bay Colony Charter required a convening of the General Court four times a year, whereas Winthrop had convened it only once each year. When the freemen discovered what the Charter really said, they voted to depose Winthrop and replace him with the deputy governor, Thomas Dudley. Historian Paul Johnson calls this incident "the first political coup in the history of North America."[21] Winthrop's deposition was voted for by the freemen of the colony not only because of his high-handedness in not convening the General Court but also because he had insisted on oaths of personal loyalty to him as governor and had frequently acted autocratically.

The new administration of Dudley and his associates wasted little time before deciding in October 1635 to arrest Roger Williams and deport him to England. It was his close friendship with Winthrop and the fact that Winthrop was no longer the governor that saved him. Winthrop was aware of what had been decided in council, so he secretly sent word to warn Williams to flee from the Bay Colony to Providence, in what is now Rhode Island. It was a narrow and harrowing escape, for Williams had to flee from Plymouth, where he had been a preacher, in the snows of winter.

The confrontation of the Bay Colony leadership with Williams was followed shortly afterward by the Anne Hutchinson affair. She had arrived in the colony as an immigrant in 1634 and was heavily influenced by the preacher John Cotton. She was a highly intelligent woman and a gifted speaker. Before long, she was conducting prayer meetings first for women, then for listeners of both sexes, in her home. Her views generally agreed with Puritan orthodoxy, but she was forceful and articulate in expressing her opinion on the need for a greater participation of women in Puritan society. Where she parted company with the Puritan preachers and civilian leaders of the colony was in her objection to sermons calling for closer obedience to civil law as a part of honoring the "second" covenant (of the community with God). She considered this emphasis as denoting a "works-based" righteousness. Christians, she felt, could sin freely without necessarily endangering their salvation.

In 1637 she was brought to a civil trial before the General Court of Massachusetts, presided over by John Winthrop, who had been re-elected governor the previous year. Though she answered the charges against her with wit and skill, it was clear that the opinion of the court was already set. What ensured that she would be found guilty was her insistence that she could determine God's will simply by listening to the Holy Spirit and without regard to God's Word, the Bible. In the views of the Puritan leadership, she was a potentially dangerous disturber of the peace. When she was excommunicated from the Puritan Church for dissenting from orthodoxy and banished from the community, she decided in March of 1638 to accept the invitation of Roger Williams to find refuge in Providence.

The weaknesses of the Puritan settlement in New England are obvious: the disdainful and sometimes criminally wrong treatment of Native Americans, the intolerance of dissenting theological views, and the quest for legalistic righteousness that inevitably often led to pride. Yet it is absurd to apply twentieth-century values—they didn't provide full liberation for women, they had slaves—to the seventeenth-century community of

Christian believers who immigrated to America. Every community in every age has glaring weaknesses, usually conferred by the social and political prejudices of the age. We often don't notice these shortcomings until the generations that exhibited them are long since departed. Yet Professors Noll, Hatch, and Marsden, in their *Search for Christian America*, make the assertion that the thoughts and actions of the Puritans in New England "do not lead to the conclusion that there was once a properly Christian nation."[22]

What is "properly Christian"? Prior to 1620 there had been no known civil compact anywhere in Christendom that involved the willing mutual submission of all the members of a community. It is clear that after the arrival of Winthrop and the Puritans in 1630, the inhabitants of the New England colonies were picking their way through the minefield of how to live a Christian life in a society comprised of sinners. They made many mistakes, especially by acting harshly towards Roger Williams and Anne Hutchinson. Yet they sought to preserve the structure of a civil community that was elected by constituent members and at the same time be reserved in making theological judgments about other members of the community. It is surely unreasonable to apply to seventeenth-century English settlers in a sometimes hostile North America the standards and values we now take for granted in our comfortable lives.

In fact, Noll, Hatch, and Marsden appear to contradict their own dismissal of the early New England settlers as not "properly Christian" when they add, a little later in their text, that "there is at least one major area where a case can be made for just such a conclusion" (that the settlers were "properly Christian"). This, they say, "is the area of general moral influence in helping to create a law-abiding citizenry with a strong conscience. . . .

Although the exact connections are impossible to document definitively, it does appear that Americans were generally well disposed to obey the civil law, to play by the rules in the democratic process and to bring their actions and those of others under moral review."[23] That sounds "properly Christian" to me. The Puritans, surely, came to have this influence because they consistently attempted to live their lives by the highest standards of Christian conduct as they perceived them to be. Christian piety rather than any other religious activity seems to have gotten them that way.

Mark Noll, a member of the trio of scholars who wrote *The Search for Christian America*, has acquired some prominence on his own through his work *The Scandal of the Evangelical Mind*, so it might be thought the phrase "properly Christian" implied in his mind intellectual acuity, whereas, by implication, the Puritans perhaps lacked this. But while evangelical Christians in contemporary America have sometimes had a reputation for not being intellectually up to snuff, whatever shortcomings the Puritans undoubtedly displayed, absence of intellect or educational attainment was not one of them. It is the consensus, in fact, of many historians that the Puritan period of American history was one of exceptional commitment by the community to the principle of learning. Harvard College, later to become Harvard University, was founded in 1636 to provide high academic training for the preachers that the Puritans wanted in their community. It is surely therefore significant that a secular historian, the late Richard Hofstadter, said of the Puritans, "It is doubtful that any community ever had more faith in the value of learning and the intellect than Massachusetts Bay. . . . Among the first generation of American puritans, men of learning were both numerous and honored. . . . These Puritan emigrants [from

England] expected their clergy to be distinguished for scholarship, and during the entire colonial period all but five percent of the clergymen of New England Congregational churches had college degrees."[24]

Nor should it be thought that Harvard College and other academic institutions that grew up during the Puritan period were narrowly focused theological factories. "In fact," Hofstadter adds, "the Oxford and Cambridge colleges which trained the men who founded Harvard College had long since been thoroughly infused with humanist scholarship. The founding fathers of colonial education saw no difference between the basic education appropriate for a cleric and that appropriate for any other liberally educated man. The idea of a distinctively theological seminary is a product of modern specialism, sectarian competition, and of a reaction to the threat of secularism in the colleges."[25] If being "properly Christian" implies warm enthusiasm for learning and academic attainment, the Puritans certainly qualified as "properly Christian."

TRAGEDIES AND FAILURES

Yet the combination of academic talent and theological zeal did not always have a happy result in Puritan New England. One of the most notorious incidents was the Salem witch trials of 1692. The basic facts of the case are not in dispute. Two young girls who were daughters of the vicar of Salem were thought to have a case of "hysteria." On investigation, they reported that they had been listening attentively to the mysterious tales of a black slave called Tituba. Under pressure of the investigation, Tituba said that she had been a "servant of Satan." The girls also implicated other members of the community, who immediately fell under suspicion of witchcraft. Hysteria over the possible presence of witches in the community led to a hasty series of investigations and the convening of a special court. Trials were held after a few months, leading to the execution of twenty people convicted of witchcraft. This sociopathology mercifully died out by October 1692, and in time the Massachusetts General Court issued an apology to the relatives of the executed and granted indemnities.

A major factor in the change of heart in Massachusetts from witch-hunting hysteria to restored common sense was the return from England of Increase Mather, a learned Puritan dignitary who was the president of Harvard College. In this affair, though, he was strongly at odds with his son Cotton Mather, a brilliant and prolific writer who had himself graduated from Harvard and was interested in medicine. Cotton Mather had a large library of books on astrology and the paranormal, and he believed in the phenomenon of witches.

The tragedy of the Salem witchcraft trials was that it was a case of mass hysteria largely fueled by political, and indeed criminal, vindictiveness on the part of less-educated laypeople. The deaths of twenty people because of hysterical public persecution were tragic, but the trials need to be kept in perspective relative to other spasms of anti-witch hysteria elsewhere. In the entire Puritan period of dominance in New England—say from 1630 to the end of the seventeenth century—there were thirty-four executions for witchcraft (including the ones at Salem). In Scotland during the same period, by contrast, there were one hundred times as many executions for witchcraft.[26] Some historians have noted how rapidly and completely the Puritan establishment admitted the error of their earlier hysteria and offered apology and compensation to their victims. "What strikes the historian, however," writes one commentator, "is not just the intensity of the self-delusion, by no means unusual for the age, but the speed of the recovery from it in the autumn [of 1692], and the anxiety of the local government and society to confess wrongdoing, to make reparation and search for the truth. That indeed was uncommon in any age. In the late 17th century it was perhaps more remarkable than the hysteria itself and a good augury for America's future as a humane and truth-seeking commonwealth."[27] Perhaps "the area of general moral influence in helping to create a law-abiding citizenry with a strong conscience"—the area of Puritan moral worth conceded by the Noll-Hatch-Marsden team—was most clearly in evidence in the speed with which the injustices and misjudgments of the Salem witch trials were reversed.

By the end of the seventeenth century the spiritual enthusiasm of many of the original Puritan settlers and their families had dimmed somewhat. In addition, the increasing wealth of all the colonies sometimes tended either to crowd out religious zeal or to temper it with the trappings of prosperity and respectability. The European Enlightenment, though not yet in full flower, was also progressively altering the theological landscape of New England. Deism and Unitarianism were beginning to make an appearance, particularly in New England. In addition, the morals and habits of young people were being affected by some local customs that caught on in New England families. One of them was "bundling," which was the sleeping together in the same bed of young people of the opposite sex, partially clothed, and with the permission of the parents. It was supposed to enable young people to get to know each other better. It certainly did this, but not surprisingly, it also created an increase in unplanned pregnancies.[28]

THE GREAT AWAKENING

It was in this setting that the pastor of a Congregationalist Church in Northampton, Massachusetts, Jonathan Edwards, became the herald of a widespread movement of local-level evangelism that became known as the Great Awakening. Edwards is widely regarded as one of the first-rate minds in the whole of American history, and he believed passionately in God's grace and the need for personal conversion. He also clearly believed that America—or at least the New England colonies of his day—had a Christian destiny. The author of several books on various aspects of God's mercy and goodness, he has become most famous in history for his sermon "Sinners in the Hands of an Angry God." In it he spoke of "the God that holds you over the pit of hell, much as one holds a spider, or some loathsome insect, over the fire, abhors you, and is dreadfully provoked."[29]

The intent of this sermon, of course, was to provoke his listeners to repentance and to a change of life, but it would be wrong to imagine that Edwards was morbidly preoccupied with God's wrath. He was concerned with what he considered a general decline in religious seriousness and the excessive partying of young people. He preached against both vigorously. In 1733 a religious revival broke out, then spread to other towns, and by the end of the decade much of New England had been transformed because of the dramatic effect it had on people's lifestyles. Edwards was fascinated by the fruits of personal conversion, and he wrote the book *A Faithful Narrative* to describe specific conversions in his own parish. Yet the real power of the Great Awakening to arouse whole communities was not fully seen until the visit of English evangelist George Whitefield in 1739 and 1740. In many respects the conviction that America indeed had a "Christian" destiny grew out of the New England revivals presided over by Whitefield.

In 1739 Whitefield preached to crowds of several thousand people up and down the East Coast of America. In one of the more unusual friendships of the eighteenth century in America, Whitefield became very close to one of the American Revolution's most famous figures, Benjamin Franklin. Franklin, of course, was a Deist and in no way enthusiastic for Whitefield's theology. But he had seen Whitefield successfully address with his unassisted voice an audience of eight thousand people in Philadelphia and believed that he was capable of being heard by up to thirty thousand. The author of *Poor Richard's Almanac* disagreed with Whitefield's theology—Franklin never moved on to orthodox Christian belief from his Deism—but, having come out of a Puritan background in his childhood, strongly supported the morality and sense of fair play that he felt the Puritans had brought to America. Franklin believed in a God who guided the affairs of nations, and Franklin was a strong supporter of religion as a guide to moral behavior. To support Whitefield, Franklin published all of Whitefield's sermons and journals. He also provided a witty account of Whitefield's skill as a speaker, admitting that he had been seduced by Whitefield's oratory into contributing far more to a church collection plate than he had intended.[30]

Whitefield's preaching in the open air did not derive from his being a compulsive outdoorsman. Because of his exclusion from many churches in North America, Whitefield took to preaching in fields, marketplaces, and other open areas, complete with a portable folding oak pulpit. This earned him the moniker of a "mob preacher," meaning that he was reaching out to all the rougher segments of society as well as to its respectable members.

The Great Awakening displeased much of the ecclesiastical establishment of the Congregational Church in New England. Though Whitefield was an ordained member of the Church of England, its senior prelates disapproved of Whitefield's dramatic and often emotional preaching style. The Congregationalists, far more numerous than the Anglicans in Massachusetts, closed the doors of their churches to him and his like-minded fellow evangelists. Those who supported Edwards and his evangelicalism were called by contemporaries "New Lights," while those who opposed it were called "Old Lights." New converts to Edwards's zealous evangelistic approach to life were often called, on both sides of the Atlantic, "enthusiasts." The term had a connotation as equally derogatory as the term "fundamentalist" when employed today to negatively label evangelical Christians. Edwards was recognized as a brilliant thinker and expositor of Christian doctrine, but he was the target of sharp and sometimes intemperate criticism from his clerical colleagues even though he brought masses of previously unchurched Americans into the habits of Bible reading, democratic assembly led by laypeople, and an indifference to social hierarchy that was far-reaching in its impact.

In the nineteenth century, historians began to acknowledge that there had indeed been a great religious stirring in New England in the decades from 1730 onwards, the first acknowledgment of the Great Awakening. It was then an easy leap to the view that the Great Awakening might have had an important role in preparing Americans for the ordeal of the struggle for independence from England. The revival taught vigorously that all men were equal and in equal need of salvation, and it encouraged Americans to make their own judgments about their faith based on their reading of the Bible. Harvard historian Alan

Heimert argues in *Religion and the American Mind* that the spirit of the Great Awakening became the vital force behind the American Revolution. "Calvinism," says Heimert, "and Edwards provided pre-Revolutionary America with a radical, and even democratic and social ideology, and evangelical religion embodied, and inspired, a thrust towards American nationalism."[31]

HOW CHRISTIAN?

When the argument about the state of American Christianity at the time of the American Revolution comes up, it falls into four general categories:

1. How many Americans attended church at the time of the Revolution?
2. How "Christian" was the behavior of Americans, given that the vice of slavery was widely practiced in America?
3. How many, and which, of the Founders were evangelical or at least self-consciously professing and outspoken Christians?
4. How much "Christian" content is in the founding documents?

Noll, Hatch, and Marsden, the most evangelical of the skeptics on the issue of the degree of "Christianness" in the American colonies at the time of the Revolution, make several points. They argue, for example, that church membership may never have amounted to more than one third of the New England population, and that in some of the southern counties it probably did not rise above 5 percent. They also argue that the Revolutionary period "was marked by declining concern for church, weakness in evangelicalism, and general spiritual lassitude. Not until the local revivals in Virginia and Connecticut in the 1780s, which anticipated the Second Great Awakening in the early 1800s, did Christianity show marked gains in the new United States." Finally, they make the important point that the closest followers of Jonathan Edwards disagreed strongly with many of the views of the patriots for the understandable reason that the patriots seemed to care much about their own freedom but not at all for that of American slaves.[32]

The view of Christian fervor in decline at the time of the Revolution, however, is strongly disputed by other authorities. According to James Hutson, chief of the manuscript division of the Library of Congress and author of several works on the Revolutionary period, the view that religion by 1700 had reached a sort of decline, which may not have been permanently reversed by the Great Awakening, is incorrect. It is not true, Hutson says, that religion had died out by 1700 or had basically acquiesced to the views of the Enlightenment by the time of the Revolution. Hutson continues, "This view is wrong, say recent authorities: according to one expert, religion in the eighteenth century was actually in the 'ascension rather than the declension' and another scholar sees a 'rising vitality in religious life' from 1700 onward; a third goes even further and finds religion in many parts of the colonies in a state of 'feverish growth.'"[33]

The issue of the acceptance of the existence of slavery by most of the patriots is an important failing of their collective Christian conscience. There were, of course, patriots who vociferously opposed slavery, and did so after the Revolution had been won and the latest question in dispute was the nature of the United States Constitution. But the general blindness to the evil of slavery reflects a broadly accepted social convention of the time, deplorable though it may be to us, in much the same way that most of the Christian world accepted the general imposition of limits to the public role of women until acceptance in the twentieth century of women's rights to vote and to be involved in politics.

FAITH OF THE FOUNDERS

One of the most detailed recent studies of the one hundred or so men who signed either the Declaration of Independence, the Constitution, or both is contained in Michael Novak's *On Two Wings*. He writes,

> Virtually all the signers of the Declaration and the Constitution were churchgoing men. Several were ministers or chaplains, others had trained to become ministers, and still others were conspicuously learned in religion. Of the 56 signers of the Declaration, 34 were Anglican, 13 were Congregationalist (once known as Puritans), 6 Presbyterian, and one each Baptist, Catholic, and Quaker. The proportions regarding the Constitution were nearly the same.[34]

Without question, some of the founders were ardent evangelical Christians and earnestly desired to be part of the founding of a Christian nation. Among the most conspicuous, of course, was Patrick Henry of Virginia. According to Thomas Kidd, author of *God of Liberty: A Religious History of the American Revolution*, "revolutionary writers and orators like Patrick Henry and even religious skeptics like Tom Paine self-consciously employed an evangelical style to motivate their audiences."[35] It was true then, as it is today, that ordinary people could be moved by evangelical rhetoric without themselves subscribing to evangelical Christian belief. Yet Kidd argues that not only Henry's verbal style but also his beliefs about liberty "arose from the Great Awakening. Henry and other Patriots, even if they might not have been ardent church-goers, sometimes absorbed in a rhetorical sense Protestant idea of resistance that would directly influence the American Revolution."[36]

What held together the wide variety of founders, despite the variety of their degrees of belief or unbelief in Christian orthodoxy, was, first, the view that in some respects Providence had been at work in the midst of their struggle to constitute a new republic. Americans, many patriots felt and said, constituted "a new Israel," a special people marked out by Providence for future greatness. Second, Americans shared a conviction that freedom of conscience was bestowed on all human beings by the Almighty. Third, many Americans at the time of the Revolution felt that the future safety of the republic they were making would be dependent on the virtue of the citizenry.

It was the avowed Deist Benjamin Franklin who articulated the providential aspect of the American Revolution. In 1784 he said, "If it had not been for the justice of our cause, and the consequent interposition of providence, in which we had faith, we must have been ruined" in the Revolution.[37] The leader of the American Revolutionary armies and America's first president, George Washington, was reticent about his personal Christian beliefs. He was an Anglican, but along with many Anglicans of his day, when he went to church he did not take communion. But Washington was not reluctant to bring Providence into his explanations for the success of the Revolution. On being appointed, reluctantly, the commander-in-chief of the Continental Army in 1776, Washington confided in a letter to his wife Martha that "It [had] been a kind of destiny that has thrown me upon this service. . . . I shall rely, therefore, confidently on that Providence which has heretofore preserved and been bountiful to me."[38]

In his first Thanksgiving proclamation after becoming president in 1789, Washington called the people of the United States "to the Service of that Great and glorious being, who is the beneficent Author of all the good that was, that is, or that will be."[39] This was a formulation that might sound unnecessarily grandiloquent to most people today, but it was certainly recognizable to any churchgoing Christians as falling within Christian doctrinal orthodoxy. Washington never spelled out the extent of his Christian beliefs, but when he wrote to the Hebrew congregation of Savannah, Georgia, in response to their congratulations on his inauguration as president, possibly in the year 1789, Washington clearly identified "Providence" as the God of the Hebrews in the Bible. In fact, Washington specifically identified Americans as heirs to the chosen people whom Moses led out of Egypt into the Promised Land. "May the same wonder-working Deity, who long since delivering the Hebrews from their Egyptian oppressors planted them in the promised land—whose Providential Agency has lately been conspicuous in establishing these United States as an independent Nation—still continue to water them with the dews of Heaven and to make the inhabitants of every denomination participate in the temporarily and spiritual blessings of that people whose God is Jehovah."[40]

The most forceful and influential articulation of the view of Providence as being involved in America's Revolution was that given by John Witherspoon, then president of Princeton, on May 17, 1776. His sermon became famous soon after its delivery and was reprinted and distributed in more than five hundred Presbyterian churches throughout the colonies. His view of Providence was sophisticated and has parallels, according to scholar Michael Novak, with that of Thomas Aquinas. The doctrine of Providence, Witherspoon said in the sermon, "extends not only to things which we may think of great moment, and therefore worthy of notice, but to things the most indifferent and inconsiderable." Witherspoon said he thought that Providence didn't manipulate people like puppets but operated through the vagaries of nature. Thus, he said, an enemy might be rendered irresolute through the assault on its commanding general of a bout of dysentery. Witherspoon added, "I think I may say with truth that there is hardly any step which they [the British] have taken, if it has operated strongly against themselves, and been more in our favor, than if they had followed a contrary course."[41]

John Adams, the second president and in many ways the architect of American independence, began his professional career with the intention of possibly becoming a clergyman. His theology became less evangelical with the passage of time, however, and though an ardent churchgoer, he ended his days as a Unitarian. Adams nevertheless subscribed to a providential view of America's beginnings. "I always consider the settlement of America with reverence and wonder," he wrote, "as the opening of a grand scene and design in Providence for the illumination of the ignorant, and the emancipation of the slavish part of mankind over all the earth."[42] Despite the steady erosion of his faith in Christian evangelical principles, Adams remained a consistent champion of the Christian faith as a bulwark of right behavior in society. "The Christian religion," he wrote in his diary on July 26, 1796, "is above all the religions that ever prevailed or existed in ancient or modern times, the religion of wisdom, virtue, equity, and humanity. . . . It is resignation to God, it is goodness itself to man."[43]

John Adams's cousin Samuel Adams was more outspokenly evangelical as the events developed that led to the American Declaration of Independence. But it is interesting that even before Thomas Jefferson penned the document, Samuel Adams was expressing a natural law version of a Creator God much closer to the Deist concept of God—which was Jefferson's at the time—than to common evangelical usage. "All men," he said, "are equally bound by the laws of nature, or to speak more properly, the laws of the Creator. They are imprinted by the finger of God on the heart of man . . . and confirmed by written revelation."[44] Thus Jefferson's wording of the Declaration—"we hold these truths to be self-evident, that all men are created equal, and they are endowed by their Creator with certain unalienable rights, that among these are Life, Liberty, and the pursuit of Happiness"—was a politically realistic blend of several streams of the religious thought of the Revolutionary generation, from committed Christian to Deist.

Samuel Adams actually signed the Declaration, as most of the delegates to the convention did, on August 2, 1776. After signing but before leaving Philadelphia, he made an impromptu speech that expressed his own view of the independence struggle in theological terms. He declared, "We have this day restored the Sovereign to whom alone men ought to be obedient. He reigns in Heaven, and with a propitious eye beholds his subjects assuming that freedom . . . which he bestowed on them. From the rising to the setting sun, may His kingdom come."[45]

The concept of liberty as a God-given quality was not limited to the thinking of evangelicals or theologically conservative Christians. Virtually all the founders believed that the Jewish and Christian religions were the principal foundations of republican liberties. Thomas Jefferson, who described himself as a Unitarian follower of Jesus but was really either a Unitarian (in his later years) or a Deist, said, "And can the liberties of a nation be thought secure when we have removed their only firm basis, a conviction in the minds of the people that these liberties are the gift of God? That they are not to be violated but with his wrath?"[46]

In Kidd's view in *God of Liberty*, some "Patriots posited an almost unbreakable link between Christianity and republican government—a bond best articulated by leading Patriot and physician Benjamin Rush of Philadelphia."[47] After the adoption of the Constitution, Rush said, "The only foundation for a republic is to be laid in Religion. Without this there can be no virtue, and without virtue there can be no liberty, and liberty is the object and life of all republican governments."[48] But Rush became more liberal in his theological views and eventually became a Universalist (someone who believes everyone will be saved, whether Christian not).

There was enormous variety in the theological views of the supporters of the American Revolution in New England from evangelical through Deist. What all proponents of American independence held in common in their theology, however, was the conviction that America, in its rebellion against perceived tyranny, now had a special compact with the Almighty.

One of Boston's most conspicuously liberal pastors (from a theological perspective) was Jonathan Mayhew, pastor of West Church in Boston. Mayhew was quite theological in his support of America's revolution, deeming it a "glorious" Christian duty to resist tyranny.[49] America's Tories (those who wanted the independence rebellion suppressed), meanwhile, identified religious affections themselves as a leading cause of the rebellion against George III. They particularly denounced local New England clergymen for allowing themselves to become the dupes, as they thought, of incendiaries like Samuel Adams. These observers concluded that certain of the colonies' religious denominations were, by doctrine and tradition, inherently subversive and could never coexist with monarchical government.[50] Thomas Jefferson, the favorite president of many Americans, would have agreed with this Tory complaint. "Pulpit oratory" he said constituted "'a shock of electricity' through the whole colony."[51] A British agent in New York in March of 1776 concluded that "at Bottom [this] was very much a religious war." James Hutson cites a British historian, J. C. D. Clark, who has called the American Revolution "the last great war of religion in the western world."[52]

Twentieth-century observers of the great sequence of events that led not only to the Declaration of Independence but also to the drafting and signing of the Constitution of the United States often claim to see a continuum reflecting the hand of the Almighty. These two documents, such scholars and observers argue, reveal evidence that Christianity played a major role in shaping the thinking of America at the moments it formally became a nation. Yet many historians have noted a sharp difference between the "Christian components" of the mood of the Continental Congress, which provided legislative authority for the implementation of the Constitution in 1789, and the Constitutional Convention itself. It is hard to dispute the point that the Continental Congress was significantly more alert to spiritual issues than the Constitutional Convention, even though the man charged with drafting the Declaration of Independence, Thomas Jefferson, was not even an orthodox Christian.

The first Continental Congress, meeting from September to late October of 1774, consisted of fifty-six delegates from twelve colonies who met in response to British reprisals against the

Boston Tea Party and were determined to discuss collectively their grievances against Great Britain. The second Congress, which convened in Philadelphia on May 10, 1775, was assembling after the clashes at Lexington and Concord. The War of Independence had already begun, and people's lives were in serious danger. It was, of course, under the auspices of the second Congress that the Declaration of Independence was signed.

The Congress's first appeal to its constituents was on June 12, 1775, when it called for a national day of "public humiliation, fasting and prayer," set to begin five weeks later, on July 20. Throughout the Continental Congress's life before the Constitution was adopted, the several subsequent fast days (usually in March of every year) and Thanksgiving Day (usually in late summer) proclamations showed, in the view of one historian, "how Congress, guided by covenant theology, drew the roadmap for regaining God's favor. The first requirement was that the American people recognize God's overruling Providence."[53]

The Continental Congress was particularly concerned for the godly demeanor of the army. The Articles of War governing the conduct of the Continental Army, adopted on June 30, 1775, and revised and expanded on September 20, 1776, devoted three of the four articles in the first section to the religious nurture of the troops.[54] James Hutson writes, "It is difficult to overemphasize Congress's concern for the spiritual condition of the armed forces, for the covenant mentality convinced it that irreligion in the ranks was, of all places, the most dangerous, for God might directly punish a backsliding military with defeat, extinguishing in the process American independence."[55] Congress expressed anxiety in the fast day proclamation of December 11, 1776, recommending "in the most earnest manner" to "officers civil and military under them, the exercise of repentance and reformation; and further, require of them the strict observation of the articles of war, and particularly that part of the said article, which forbids profane swearing, and all immorality."[56]

Washington himself paid special attention to the demeanor of the troops, asking officers to conduct prayers with the men. His first order as commander of the Continental Army was against blasphemy, drunkenness, and gambling. On July 4, 1775, Washington issued an order "that most earnestly requires and expects a due observance of those articles of war established for the government of the army, which forbid profane cursing, swearing, and drunkenness. And in like manner he requires and expects of all the officers and soldiers, not engaged in actual duty; a punctual attendance on Divine service, to implore the blessing of Heaven upon the means used for our safety and defense."[57]

Does this suggest that Washington and the members of the Continental Congress were unusually pious? Not at all. It simply means that, even though church attendance may have been rather low at the time of the Revolution and very few Americans were strict Calvinists in their theology, the lessons of covenant theology were deeply rooted in most Americans of that day who considered themselves Christian. Whether they attended church faithfully or not, most of them readily took to the idea that God has a special purpose for America. Was the country "exceptional"? Americans at the time of the Revolution probably would have been unsure of that particular term, but many of them felt that it probably was, by divine providence.

Virtue was a concept of classical antiquity that was not very different from Christian concepts of selflessness and truthfulness. James Hutson, the Library of Congress historian we have already encountered, believes that the revolutionary generation often conflated virtue itself with Christian morality and assumed that virtue was best promoted by Christianity. Hutson writes: "The following syllogism imprinted itself so strongly on the minds of the Founders that it became a cliché: religion promoted virtue; virtue promoted republicanism; religion promoted, and was indispensable for republicanism. In the words of Benjamin Rush (1745–1813), Christianity was 'the strong ground of republicanism . . . many of its concepts have for their objects republican liberty and equality as well as simplicity, integrity, and economy in government.'" Timothy Dwight, who was to become the president of Yale College and repeatedly warned Yale students and church audiences against the dangers of the "infidel philosophy" of the French Revolution, said of Christian moral and religious instructions, "It makes good men and good men must be good citizens."[58]

Several in the revolutionary generation were quick to draw the connection between moral behavior and the traditional Christian belief in rewards and punishments in the afterlife. Irenaeus, a Revolutionary-era editorialist who used the name of an early church father, wrote in 1780 that "the belief in future state of rewards and punishments" was absolutely "necessary for the well being of civil society," for "we shall find that persons are often restrained from gross immoralities by the fear of future miseries, when civil penalties prove insufficient for that purpose."[59] Indeed, as one of the best informed historians on religion in the revolutionary period points out, "The Christian system of behavioral incentives/disincentives seemed to be so essential for the maintenance of social order that several states—Pennsylvania (1776), Vermont (1777), South Carolina (1778) and Tennessee (1796)—prohibited individuals from voting or holding office who denied a future state of rewards and punishments."[60] A writer in the *Virginia Independent Chronicle* of 1784 editorialized: "Mankind [*sic*] have generally speaking, enacted laws to restrain and punish enormities, to countenance virtue and discourage vice: yet the most approved and wisest legislators in all ages, in order to give efficacy to their civil institutions, have found it necessary to call in the aid of religion; and in no form of government whatever has the influence of religious principles been found so requisite as in that of a republic."[61]

There was an almost universal agreement among the founders on what constituted virtue and what constituted vice, regardless of the differences among them on points of strict theology. This explains the apparent oddity of Thomas Jefferson's behavior. A Deist with sympathies for some of the most radical ideas of the French Revolution in the late 1780s and the 1790s, when president he became one of the most ardent of America's chief executives ever to encourage churchgoing as a civic virtue. Some people believe that Jefferson underwent a sort of conversion to Unitarian Christianity after reading in 1793 a book by Joseph Priestley, *A History of the Corruptions of Christianity*. In any event, Jefferson was not shy in openly saying that he was a Christian: "I am a Christian," he wrote to Benjamin Rush in 1803, "in the only sense in which he [Jesus] wished any one to be: sincerely attached to his doctrines, in preference to all others; ascribing to himself every human excellence; and believing he never claimed other."[62]

During his presidency, Jefferson assiduously attended church services in the original chamber of the House of Representatives in the Capitol. One anecdote about his allegedly being challenged by a clergyman who encountered him en route to the church service is revealing. "You going to church?" the Reverend

Ethan Allen reportedly asked Jefferson. "You do not believe a word in it." Jefferson did not contradict the comment but responded, "No nation has ever yet existed or been governed without religion. Nor can be. The Christian religion is the best religion that has ever been given to man and I as chief Magistrate of this nation am bound to give it the sanction of my example. Good morning, Sir."[63]

The church services held in the Capitol, with Jefferson regularly attending, were by today's standards surprisingly ecumenical. Preachers on any Sunday ranged from denominations such as Anglicans or Presbyterians, Swedenborgians, Quakers, Unitarians, Baptists, and even Roman Catholics. James Hutson emphasizes how significant it was that Jefferson helped make federal government property available for different church groups. "It is no exaggeration to say that, on Sundays in Washington during Thomas Jefferson's presidency, the state became the church."[64] In January of 1806, Jefferson and fellow congregants listened to a thunderous message on the need to be "born again" from Dorothy Ripley, an English preacher who traveled across the Atlantic several times to evangelize the Americans. Apparently no great fuss was made about the fact that a woman was preaching in the church, but when the House of Representatives elected a Unitarian as chaplain and invited him to preach in 1821, an Episcopalian priest complained that the Unitarian had "expelled Jesus Christ from the House."[65]

How does the striking evidence of Jefferson's approval of the use of federal property for Christian church services square with the famous and much-quoted Jefferson pronouncement, in a letter to the Danbury Baptist Association in January 1802, on the need for "a wall of separation" between church and state? In the letter, frequently cited by the Supreme Court in the twentieth century, Jefferson made it clear that he did not proclaim fasts and thanksgivings as his predecessors in office, including George Washington, had done. The speculation is that, while making a philosophical statement that justified his refusal to announce national religious events, Jefferson didn't want to alienate pious New England Christians who had helped vote him into office. Accordingly, two days after writing to the Danbury Baptists, Jefferson attended church in the House of Representatives, and he was a regular and frequent church attender for the remainder of his presidency.[66]

Jefferson had campaigned for the presidency in 1800 in the face of harsh accusations from political opponents that he was an "infidel" and even an atheist. If he ever had been such, he certainly wasn't by the time he became president. On New Year's Day in 1802 he had received at the White House a gift of a gigantic block of cheese, weighing 1,235 pounds in all, from Cheshire, Massachusetts, on the instructions of a leading evangelical Baptist of the day, Rev. John Leland. Many Baptists, including Leland, had supported Jefferson for the presidency in the election of 1800 because they deemed that a political alliance with a suspected Deist was the best guarantee for religious freedom for Baptists. As late as the 1770s, Baptists in Virginia, a predominantly Anglican state, had been not only dunked in water in mockery of the rite of baptism but in at least one instance actually beaten to death. Historian Thomas Kidd writes that the cheese symbolized one of the strangest, but most significant political and cultural alliances of the early post-Independence nation: "an unlikely alliance of evangelicals, Enlightenment liberals, and deists, working together to win religious freedom."[67]

That religious freedom, of course, did not become protected by federal law until the ratification of the First Amendment to the Constitution in 1789. But the Constitutional Convention itself reflected a very different mood—one of self-confidence in the ability of the new nation to survive—from the Continental Congresses that had issued countless calls to prayer and fasting in the 1770s. In fact, several attendees of the Convention, as well as others, complained that despite the apparently divine blessing on the American Revolutionary effort, the Constitution itself made no reference to the Almighty. "Many pious people," Benjamin Rush said to John Adams in 1789, "wish the name of the Supreme Being had been introduced somewhere in the new Constitution." Timothy Dwight, the president of Yale, observed, "We found the Constitution without any acknowledgment of God; without any recognition of his mercies to us . . . or even of his existence. The Convention, by which it was formed, never asked, even once, his direction of his blessing upon their labours."[68]

Many Americans since the time of the Constitution have been puzzled in the same way. It is revealing that Benjamin Franklin, the oldest delegate to the Constitutional Convention, reproved his fellow delegates on June 28, 1787, soon after the Constitutional Convention opened in Philadelphia, for forgetting "their powerful Friend" (God) who had helped guide the Americans to victory. "I have lived a long time," Franklin told the Convention, "and the longer I live, the more convincing proofs I see of this Truth—*that God governs in the affairs of men*. . . . We have been assured, Sir, in the Sacred Writings, that 'except the Lord build the house, they labour in vain that build it.' I firmly believe this; and I also believe that, without his concurrent Aid, we shall succeed in this Political building no better than the Builders of Babel." Franklin, consistent with his comments, moved that "Prayers, imploring the Assistance of Heaven, and its blessing on our Deliberations, be held in this Assembly every morning." The motion failed, possibly because the Convention did not possess funds to pay a chaplain.[69]

Toward the end of the Convention, however, sentiment in favor of a thanksgiving proclamation surfaced once more. On September 25, 1789, Elias Boudinot, a member of the Continental Congress and later the first House of Representatives, told his fellow delegates to the Convention that "he could not think of letting the session pass over without offering an opportunity to all the citizens of the United States of joining, with one voice, in returning to Almighty God their sincere thanks for the many blessings that He poured down upon them." Boudinot moved that the House and Senate request the president "to recommend to the people of the United States a day of public thanksgiving and prayer, to be observed by acknowledging, with grateful hearts, the many signal favors of Almighty God."

Only two congressmen went on record as opposing Boudinot's motion, both of whom took the position that Congress was prescribed from doing this by the Bill of Rights it had just passed. Congressman Roger Sherman responded that examples of national thanksgiving had precedents in "Holy Writ," in itself a comment that implied, without anyone's contradicting him, that "Holy Writ" was an accepted belief of the vast majority of the Congress. In consequence, on October 3, 1789, George Washington issued a proclamation recommending that the American people thank God on November 26 for "his single and manifold mercies, and the favorable interpositions of his providence" as well as plead with God to "pardon our national and other transgressions."[70]

Washington, as we have seen, was not at all a Deist but believed that God answered prayer and that Christian behavior was a prerequisite for decent republican society and government. In his farewell address to the American people on September 19, 1796, Washington delivered his most famous—and frequently quoted—pronouncement on the subject. The speech was originally drafted by Alexander Hamilton, but the final version of it was Washington's. He wrote,

> Of all the dispositions and habits which lead to political prosperity, religion and morality are indispensable supports. In vain would that man claim the tribute of patriotism, who should labor to subvert these great pillars of human happiness, these firmest props of the duties of men and citizens. The mere politician, equally with the pious man, ought to respect and to cherish them. A volume could not trace all their connections with private and public felicity. Let it be simply asked: Where is the security for property, for reputation, for life, if the sense of religious obligation desert the oaths which are the instruments of investigation in courts of justice? And let us with caution indulge the supposition that morality can be maintained without religion. Whatever may be conceded to the influence of refined education on minds of peculiar structure, reason and experience both forbid us to expect that national morality can prevail in exclusion of religious principle.
>
> It is substantially true that virtue or morality is a necessary spring of popular government. The rule, indeed, extends with more or less force to every species of free government. Who that is a sincere friend to it can look with indifference upon attempts to shake the foundation of the fabric?[71]

The farewell address, of course, has traditionally been closely examined to discern what Washington's major political concerns may have been for the future stability of the independent American state. For example, many commentators have focused on Washington's injunction to the country he had just finished governing to "steer clear of permanent alliances with any portion of the foreign world" and have thereby been emboldened to criticize key American alliances since World War II such as NATO. But probably a more fundamental precept on behavior toward foreign nations is contained in these words:

> Observe good faith and justice towards all nations; cultivate peace and harmony with all. Religion and morality enjoin this conduct; and can it be, that good policy does not equally enjoin it—It will be worthy of a free, enlightened, and at no distant period, a great nation, to give to mankind the magnanimous and too novel example of a people always guided by an exalted justice and benevolence. Who can doubt that, in the course of time and things, the fruits of such a plan would richly repay any temporary advantages which might be lost by a steady adherence to it? Can it be that Providence has not connected the permanent felicity of a nation with its virtue? The experiment, at least, is recommended by every sentiment which ennobles human nature. Alas! Is it rendered impossible by its vices?[72]

Washington's immediate successor, John Adams, was a man of evolving theology who nevertheless described himself as a churchgoing man. But as Washington had done before him, and Jefferson was to do after him, Adams gave strong rhetorical support to religion. "Statesmen may plan and speculate for Liberty," he said, "but it is Religion and Morality alone, which can establish the principles upon which Freedom can securely stand."[73] In his inaugural address, Adams said that he considered "a decent respect for Christianity among the best recommendations for public service."[74] He was careful, however, not to suggest that this amounted to a necessary qualification for political responsibility, which would have been in contradiction of Article Six of the Constitution that there be "no religious test." Adams continued as president the fast-day proclamations that the Continental Congress had initiated. When war seemed imminent between the United States and France in 1798, Adams issued a proclamation for a fast on March 23 of that year. The country, he thought, once again needed to repent. "All religious congregations," he said, ought "with the deepest humility, acknowledge before God the manifold sins and transgressions with which we are justly charged as individuals and as a nation; beseeching Him at the same time, of His infinite grace, through the Redeemer of the World, freely to remit all our offences, and to incline us, by His Holy Spirit to that sincere repentance and reformation which may afford us reason to hope for his inestimable favor and heavenly benediction."[75] War was narrowly avoided. Someone, perhaps, was listening.

After Adams, Thomas Jefferson was, as we have already noticed, a demonstrative public supporter of religion, whether or not he personally believed Christian doctrines. More than any other early American president, he was fascinated by the person and teachings of Jesus, even if he considered many Christian beliefs, such as the virgin birth of Jesus, to be mere fables. Long after he had stepped down from the presidency, Jefferson in retirement at Monticello worked on what became known as the *Jefferson Bible* or, more formally, *The Life and Morals of Jesus of Nazareth*. The manuscript was never published in Jefferson's lifetime, and only in the past decade has the manuscript become available for public scrutiny at the Smithsonian's National Museum of American History in Washington, DC. In essence, Jefferson took a sharp knife to the text of the four Gospels and compiled his own narrative from the text, making sure that he literally cut out any parts of the Gospel narrative that referred to miraculous events.

Jefferson's successor in the office of the presidency, James Madison, is historically significant for American religion because he was not only the "Father of the Constitution" but the "Father of the First Amendment," which both protects Americans from government imposition of religious practices and beliefs and protects citizens in their right to choose whichever way they want to worship or not worship (the "free exercise" clause). Madison, however, had already played a historically significant role in the shaping of American religious practice when, in the Virginia General Assembly in 1784, he opposed a bill by Virginia legislator Patrick Henry "establishing a Provision for Teachers of the Christian religion." The bill was nondiscriminatory and merely asked citizens to pay a tax to support the religious denomination of their choice. In fact, it would have brought Virginia in line with many other colonies that had supported the established church with the financial assistance of the state until well into the nineteenth century.

But the odd-couple alliance of evangelical Baptists with theologically liberal Christians and Deists, already mentioned above in relation to the Jefferson-John Leland alliance, was adamantly opposed to the Patrick Henry bill. Opponents of the bill believed that state establishment of religion was not far removed from the monarchical system of government that Americans had opposed in fighting for independence. Though many Virginians in 1784 supported the bill, including George Washington and John Marshall, it was derailed when its chief proponent, Patrick Henry, was sidelined from the legislature by being promoted to governor. Opposition to it was then successfully mobilized, and it was defeated in the autumn of 1785.[76]

An overwhelming majority of Americans believed in the social value of Christianity in the first few years after the Revolution, even if not all of them accepted orthodox doctrines. A few prominent Americans, after independence, were nevertheless sharply hostile to Christianity in any form. One assault on the Christian faith was Thomas Paine's *The Age of Reason*, published in 1794. This was a sharp attack on the Bible and on key Christian doctrines like the resurrection and the virgin birth, doctrines to which Jefferson himself was opposed and which came under attack in his own treatise on Christianity previously discussed.

What offended many American Christians at the time was Paine's intemperate irreverence. Paine was a Deist, not an atheist, and he had been led to go to France by his antipathy towards the atheists and the atheistic direction in which he thought the French Revolution was headed. But Paine's work briefly touched off a flurry of conspiratorial theories about unbelief in the United States as, supposedly, the product of subversive attempts of European revolutionaries to undermine both American republican democracy and Christianity. Yale's President Timothy Dwight warned darkly in 1798, "Shall our sons become the disciples of Voltaire and the dragoons of Marat or our daughters the concubines of the *Illuminati*?"[77]

REVIVAL

Dwight need not have worried. America was on the brink of a series of Christian revivals that were to extend well into the nineteenth century and were to shape the national culture decisively. The Second Great Awakening, broadly speaking, is associated with revival movements that began in Connecticut in 1797 and spread throughout New England. At Yale College, there were reported to be fifteen long-lasting revivals between 1800 and 1840.[78] The most famous outbreak of religious zeal, however, took place in Cane Ridge, Kentucky, in 1801. Up to seventy-five thousand people gathered for preaching and prayer meetings that lasted sometimes for days at a time.

These revivals apparently resulted in marked social effects. One teacher traveling in Kentucky in 1802, at the height of the revivals there, was struck by the change in manners of the region. What had once apparently been a wild and lawless place had become transformed. "I found Kentucky the most moral place I have ever been in," he said. "A religious awe seemed to pervade the country." The same change of behavior, he reported, was noticeable in South Carolina after revivals there. "Drunkards," he continued, "have become more sober and orderly—bruisers, bullies, and blackguards meek, inoffensive, and peaceable," he continued.[79]

The revivals in individual states and counties were so numerous that most researchers have abandoned the task of keeping track of them. But in addition to local revivals confined to one locality, a new phenomenon was coming into existence: the practice of "circuit riding" by itinerant pastors and evangelists, most of whom were Methodists. The necessity of circuit riding, by which a single preacher would service in turn several different pastoral communities, arose from the absence of actual church buildings or permanent organizations, especially in America's frontier regions. The precedent for traveling clergy was set by the Englishman Francis Asbury, who was the founding bishop of American Methodism. Asbury himself rode approximately 270,000 miles in a career of itinerant preaching, building up Methodist communities wherever he could. The growth of

Methodism in America was astonishingly swift. The Methodists in 1780 had fewer than 10,000 members, but by 1820 they had grown to 250,000. They numbered half a million by 1830 and by 1840 had doubled again. By 1844 they were the nation's largest denomination, with 1,068,525 members. All three major denominations—Methodists, Baptists, and Presbyterians—grew with great rapidity, almost certainly because all three were fiercely evangelical.

The phenomenon of growth among America's evangelical churches was to continue well up to the end of the century. The late professor of political science Seymour Martin Lipset cited figures indicating that Americans affiliated with evangelical Christian denominations numbered about 11,763,000 in 1856, out of a population of 26,500,000. By 1890, H. K. Carroll, who was in charge of the Division of Churches for the 1890 census, concluded that, with a total United States population in that year of 62,622,250, only five million were not communicants or adherents of a Christian denomination. In fact, he calculated that 92 percent in 1890 and 91 percent in 1910 were linked in some way to a Christian denomination.[80] There had been yet another surge of awakening around the time of the American Civil War, in both the North and the South.

Americans themselves had noticed that here and there, wherever revivals were taking place, there was a marked improvement in the manners of the people. Yet the most striking evidence that Christianity had profoundly affected the manners of people at a popular level in America was offered by the French observer of American life Alexis de Tocqueville, who was assigned by the French government as a young man to observe the prison system in America. De Tocqueville's magnum opus, *Democracy in America*, published in 1835 after his return to France, offers remarkably perceptive insights into the behavior of the entire nation. "On my first arrival in America," he wrote,

> the religious aspect of the country was the first thing that struck my attention; and the longer I stayed there, the more did I perceive the great political consequences resulting from this state of things. In France I had almost always seen the spirit of religion and the spirit of freedom pursuing courses diametrically opposed to each other, but in America I found they were intimately united, and that they reigned in common over the same country.[81]

While Alexis de Tocqueville was still in America, Charles Finney, later considered the "father of modern revivalism," emerged as one of the most effective and influential revival preachers in America in the nineteenth century. At the time of his dramatic personal conversion to Christian belief in 1821, he was a legal apprentice in Adams, New York. His interest in the Bible derived from his frequent encounters with biblical quotations in the law books he was using at work. Finney believed that successful evangelism was a product of using the right evangelistic methods. In his case, these included meticulous organization in advance of revival rallies and provision of an "anxious bench" at which sinners contemplating conversion and spiritual rebirth could be admonished to abandon their sinful life and begin anew. In 1837, Finney gave up the position of pastor at a New York church in order to become a theology professor at Oberlin College. He was very active in social movements promoting temperance, care for people with mental difficulties, coeducational college education, and the abolition of slavery.

After Asbury, Finney was certainly the most famous evangelist of the Second Great Awakening, and he set the pattern for the voluntary societies with social reform as their main intention that grew up in the wake of religious revivals. Finney embraced the new world of industrial capitalism, seamlessly blending economic success and the energetic spread of the gospel. But Finney was no advocate of capitalism in all its varieties. He forcefully opposed slavery as a great blight upon America's Christian soul. Slavery itself, of course, was not abolished in the United States until Abraham Lincoln's Emancipation Proclamation of January 1863, intended for slaves in areas under rebellion—i.e., in the South—in the midst of the American Civil War. Yet during the Civil War itself, though there were atrocities on both sides, there were also ardent Christians on both sides who believed that they were fighting in God's cause. It took Abraham Lincoln, in his second inaugural address in March 1865, to make it clear that though he judged the war itself to have been justified by the decision of the South to attempt to secede, he did not consider the South inherently more sinful in Christian terms than the North. His words were astonishingly humble and gracious toward an adversary facing imminent and total defeat, and he fully acknowledged the Christian sincerity of his foe. Among other things, he said, "Both [sides] read the same Bible and pray to the same God, and each invokes His aid against the other. . . . The prayers of both could not be answered. The prayers of neither has been answered fully. The Almighty has His own purposes." The remainder of the inaugural address makes it clear that slavery was the offense that brought on the war, but the war itself must continue until God's providential will had been entirely worked out.[82]

Lincoln tragically died barely six weeks later, before he could help "bind up the nation's wounds," but the Christian character of the nation was by now indelibly stamped into the national consciousness. The German-trained historian George Bancroft had written a narrative of American history that is often termed "magisterial," titled *History of the United States of America, from the Discovery of the American Continent*.[83] Bancroft was a committed Christian who believed in the role of God's providence in shaping the American past. He thought that America was a Christian nation established and sustained by God for the purpose of spreading liberty and democracy in the world.[84]

This seemed to be the view broadly held by a majority of America's learned elite at least through the remainder of the nineteenth century. In a remarkable case of federal prosecution of a British Anglican priest hired by New York's Church of the Holy Trinity, the Supreme Court not only took the side of the church, which was being prosecuted for violation of a law against hiring foreigners, but also stated categorically that the United States was a Christian nation. The purpose of this statement, in an opinion by Associate Justice Josiah Brewer, was not to lambast any militant atheists who may have been paying attention but to underscore the larger point that a minister of the Christian faith—no matter what denomination—was in a different category from the imported sweatshop labor that the original law of 1885 had been intended to prevent from working in the United States. The majority opinion opened with the words, "No purpose of action against religion can be imputed to any legislation, state or national, because this is a religious people. This is historically true. From the discovery of this continent to the present hour, there is a single voice making this affirmation."

The opinion then gave a survey of American history since the age of Columbus, through voyages by Sir Walter Raleigh, through the Mayflower Compact, and through the Declaration of Independence, which, the opinion goes on, "recognizes the presence of the Divine in human affairs." The opinion stated multiple times that "there is a universal language pervading them all [the previously mentioned historic events], having one meaning: they affirm and reaffirm that this is a religious nation."[85]

In case anyone had the idea that the Supreme Court thought that Americans were generally of mystical disposition because of this use of the word "religion," Justice Brewer clarified his point by referring to an earlier Supreme Court decision in *Updegraph v. Commonwealth*, a blasphemy case that reached the Supreme Court in 1824. In that decision it was decided that, continued Brewer,

> Christianity, general Christianity, is, and always has been, a part of the common law . . . not Christianity with an established church . . . but Christianity with liberty of conscience to all men. . . . If we pass beyond these matters to a view of American life as expressed by its laws, its business, its customs and society, we find everywhere a clear recognition of the same truth. Among other matters note the following: The form of oath universally prevailing, concluding with an appeal to the Almighty; the custom of opening sessions of all deliberative bodies and most conventions with prayer; the prefatory words of all wills, "In the name of God, Amen."[86]

Interestingly, Justice Brewer's opinion mentioned some customs of the United States from the most strongly Christian period of its history, such as "the observance of the Sabbath, with the general cessation of all secular assemblies on that day," which is no longer observed today and may well not have been universally observed at the time. The Supreme Court underwent some criticism for this opinion, largely from Americans who did not want to consider themselves part of a "Christian nation." In part to address these concerns, Justice Brewer published a book in 1905 called *The United States a Christian Nation*, in which he took pains to clarify his opinion:

> But in what sense can [the United States] be called a Christian nation? Not in the sense that Christianity is the established religion or that the people are in any manner compelled to support it. On the contrary, the Constitution specifically provides that 'Congress shall make no law respecting an establishment of religion, or prohibiting the free exercise thereof.' Neither is it Christian in the sense that all its citizens are either in fact or name Christians. On the contrary, all religions have free scope within our borders. Numbers of our people profess other religions, and many reject all.[87]

Brewer added that, of course, there was no religious test for office requiring people to declare themselves to be Christians.

The popular online encyclopedia Wikipedia today acknowledges that the Supreme Court decision voiced by Justice David Josiah Brewer was not in any way an attempt to enforce Christianity by law. "He was simply making," says the site, "an observation which is consistent with the fact that people in this country tend to be Christian."[88]

Brewer's brave statement about America's past, much of which would have seemed obviously true to the learned elites of America in his day, almost certainly could not have been made at any later time by any Supreme Court justice. The winds of contrary opinion had been rising for many years. By the second decade of the twentieth century, they had reached almost tornado force.

4

American Christianity and the Challenge of Modernity

The Rise of a Secular Intelligentsia

During the first two millennia of global Christendom, the watershed event was not the official adoption of Christianity by the Roman Empire under the emperor Constantine but the Protestant Reformation launched by the monk and university lecturer Martin Luther in 1517. In that year the thirty-three-year-old wrote a letter (known as *The Ninety-Five Theses*) to the bishop of Mainz protesting the sale of indulgences (the church's official remission of time that would otherwise have been spent in purgatory for sins committed) by official representatives of the pope. Luther's insistence that eternal salvation could not be earned, much less obtained on an installment plan by purchasing indulgences, but must be received by faith, through grace, set Christianity on its most dramatic path of expansion since the early church itself. Luther's challenge to the authority of the papacy was in due course punished with excommunication from the Roman Catholic Church. Protestantism, however, grew out of Luther's insistence that eternal salvation for the believer could be received only by God's grace through faith and without any intervention by the clergy.

The Reformation changed the face of Europe for all time, eventually dividing the continent after decades of brutal wars into regions and nations that were predominantly Protestant or predominantly Catholic. But it was the second stage of the Reformation, the rise of Puritanism in England and then the settlement of North America by committed Puritans, that laid the groundwork for an America that was overwhelmingly Christian in its conviction.

The high point of Christian influence in America may have been in the middle of the nineteenth century. Christianity had blossomed in the highly favorable atmosphere of economic and political freedom, and it probably reached its apogee in America during the Second Great Awakening, generally estimated to have begun at the very end of the eighteenth century and to have lasted at least until about 1850 (though there were important Christian evangelical revivals in the Confederate army during the Civil War and a dramatic urban revival in the north of the United States that began in 1858).

The expression of Christianity at that time was overwhelmingly Protestant right up until the end of the nineteenth century. American Christians often gave the impression to visiting foreigners of being not just Protestant but sometimes specifically anti-Catholic. As immigration from Europe continued to swell in the centuries that followed the Pilgrims of 1620, however, Roman Catholics became increasingly numerous and eager to form an active life of their own in their adopted nation. Between 1830 and 1860, the American population grew from 13 million to 31.5 million, but the Roman Catholic population increased nearly tenfold to 3.1 million. Inevitably, there were clashes between the Protestant and Catholic communities, and there was much ugly prejudice by Protestants against Catholics. Some of it was triggered by papal pronouncements. Pope Gregory XVI, for example, declared in an encyclical in 1832 that the Catholic Church condemned the "absurd and erroneous proposition which claims that liberty of conscience must be maintained for everyone."[1]

A prominent campaigner against the immigration into the United States of European Catholics was Samuel F. B. Morse, inventor of both the Morse code and the first successful electric telegraph. He wrote in 1835, "it is a fact that Popery is opposed in its very nature to Democratic Republicanism; and it is, therefore, as a political system, as well as religious, opposed to civil and religious liberty, and consequently, our form of government."[2] It took decades of careful work by Roman Catholic intellectuals and prelates before Catholicism was accepted by most Americans as a viable and valuable way of helping new immigrants to America to assimilate without abandoning their particular form of Christianity. Even as late as the presidential campaign of Senator John F. Kennedy in 1960, there was a last-minute attempt by some Protestant pastors to tar Kennedy with the same brush of supposed Catholic despotism as Morse and other "nativists," as they were called, had employed more than a century earlier. (The fear of a Catholic president, which

Kennedy skillfully and even elegantly addressed in Houston in 1960 before a large group of Protestant pastors, never substantively surfaced as an election issue in subsequent presidential campaigns involving a Catholic candidate.)

American Christians, of course, were also overwhelmingly white and specifically Anglo-Saxon in ethnic origin. Despite this, American blacks, even during the era of slavery, were to emerge as a force for Christian evangelism in their own right, often in the face of fierce efforts to limit their churches' prominence and growth by white American churches.

The nineteenth century in Europe gradually saw both an abandonment of Christian orthodoxy by intellectuals and the subsequent emergence of secular ideologies deeply hostile to Christianity. The new and alien ideology that was to become by far the most important among secular worldviews opposed to Christianity was Marxism-Leninism. A century and a quarter after Karl Marx wrote his *Communist Manifesto* in 1848, Marxism-Leninism had become the reigning philosophy of nations and states that accounted for nearly half the population of the world. Yet myriad other ideologies and worldviews also flourished, especially in the United States. Most Americans, even those who didn't like Christianity, came to reject Marxism-Leninism because of its association with the ugly despotism in the nations and states over which it ruled.

In the course of time, especially in the late twentieth century, these other secular philosophies—some of them heavily influenced by Marxism, but others not necessarily so—had transformed the worldview of the intellectual class in Western Europe and the United States from one that was accepting of the Christian view of life, indeed deeply supportive of it, to one that was deeply antagonistic toward Christianity.

In the course of this chapter we will examine how antagonism toward Christianity took root in North America initially among the intellectual elites of America, especially at the universities and in popular entertainment, and then filtered down to a popular level. At the beginning of the twenty-first century most Americans (about 76 percent) either thought of themselves as Christian or had generally positive feelings toward Christianity. But by the end of the first decade of the twenty-first century, popular television dramas, and especially popular comedy programs on specialized comedy television channels, were often openly hostile to the Christian worldview. Increasingly, heterosexual relationships outside marriage and romances between gay people were treated sympathetically. By contrast, characters portrayed as opposing such relationships were mocked or denigrated as bigots.

We will conclude this account of the falling away from faith with a look at the impact of the most socially turbulent decade of the twentieth century, the 1960s, on both society in general and America's colleges in particular. We should then have little difficulty in understanding to what degree the prevailing attitudes of the 1960s served to erode the core principles of social cohesion that America had taken for granted in the heyday of its Christian history.

"THE GERMAN POISON"

It was the most famous English preacher of the nineteenth century, Charles Spurgeon, who first referred to the devastating impact of philosophical developments in Germany on Christianity as "the German poison." What Spurgeon was referring to was the earth-shaking developments of philosophy in Europe, and later the United States, that really started their development with the writings of the German philosopher Friedrich Hegel. Now most Americans barely recognize the name Hegel, much less know what he was about, yet his philosophy transformed thinking in Europe in the nineteenth century and indeed underwent a renewal of its influence in the late twentieth century. Some Americans, of course, are aware that Hegel's thought had a profound influence on Karl Marx and Friedrich Engels. Far fewer know that Hegel influenced the French existentialist philosopher Jean-Paul Sartre and also such classically American figures of modern times as John Dewey. Existentialism? Isn't that some way of not being sure what you are on earth for? Sure is. But Hegel was deep in the middle of it.

Hegel's thought was so influential for a few decades that one prominent writer on philosophy has described philosophy in general in the late nineteenth and early twentieth centuries as "a series of footnotes to Hegel."[3] In recent decades, Hegel even surfaced as people contemplated the unfolding collapse of the Communist empire in Eastern Europe and the Soviet Union and the influential essay "The End of History?" by former State Department analyst Francis Fukuyama. Without Hegel, Marxism could not have come into existence. It's not a simple matter to summarize Hegel's thought, but it had an incalculable influence on the draining away of Christian belief among intellectuals in Europe and later in the United States.

There are two main parts to Hegel's view of life. First, Hegel thought of history as something that just went on relentlessly unfolding, yet in a way that showed that there was a "spirit" behind it all. (Hegel's "spirit" seemed close enough to the Christian idea of the Holy Spirit to confuse many of his readers into thinking that Hegel was some kind of Christian philosopher.)

Second, Hegel himself believed that the state was more important than individual human beings. In its early nineteenth-century Prussian authoritarian form, he suggested that the state was the culmination of how history was propelling human society into the future. This aspect of Hegel's thought has caused some atheists to hold a very critical view of Hegel. The famous atheist and British philosopher Bertrand Russell once wrote, "Hegel thought that, if enough was known about a thing to distinguish it from all other things, then all its properties could be inferred by logic. This was a mistake, and from this mistake arose the whole imposing edifice of his system. This illustrates an important truth, namely that the worse your logic, the more interesting the consequences to which it gives rise."[4] Given the fact that Hegel clearly influenced Marx and Marxism, a system with dubious consequences, as well as dangerously influential thinkers like Nietzsche (who helped give birth to German fascism in the 1930s), Russell's sardonic observation carries some weight.

Hegel began his university studies at the University of Tubingen, a center of learning noted for its skepticism toward the Bible. A prominent admirer of Hegel, the Hungarian Gyorgy Lukacs, wrote that Hegel's early attitude toward Christianity was one of "hatred and contempt" and said that such a view arose from "exaggerated expectations and longings for a revolutionary regeneration of mankind" and enthusiasm for the recently completed French Revolution.[5] Particularly offensive to Hegel was the Christian idea that human beings should submit themselves to God. He said that it was grotesque "to shudder before an unknown being; to renounce one's will in one's conduct; to subject oneself like a machine to given rules; to abandon intellect altogether in action or enunciation."[6]

Well before what Spurgeon called "the German poison" spread throughout European Christendom, the ground had been prepared for a full-scale assault on the veracity and reliability of the Bible. Voltaire, who was a critic of Christianity and the church in general but a Deist rather than an atheist or agnostic, had drawn heavily on the writings of English Deists like John Toland, Matthew Tyndal, and Anthony Collins, who still believed in the concept of God but were highly critical both of Christianity's claim to be a true revealed religion and of the various historical vices of the Christian church. Soon biblical scholars were becoming openly critical of the Bible, on the primary grounds that the alleged miracles of the Bible were simply too unlikely to have been possible.

In Germany, which was predominantly Protestant in the north of the country, the German heirs of the Enlightenment who wished to criticize Christianity and create a religion of reason to replace it focused on picking the Bible to pieces on the basis that reality itself didn't operate in the way the Bible suggested. A pathbreaking work in this vein was the *Wolfenbuttel Fragments*, a series of commentaries on the Old and New Testaments published between 1774 and 1778 and authored by a professor at the University of Hamburg, R. S. Reimarus. The most controversial part of the *Fragments*, which shocked many readers who were clergy at the time, was the last commentary, "The Aims of Jesus and Disciples." Reimarus portrayed Jesus as a ranting enthusiast who perished at the hands of the authorities because of his political ambitions. The disciples, Reimarus claimed (though he was not the first Christianity-basher to do so), had stolen the body of Jesus and devised the thus fraudulent story of the resurrection. Miracles, Reimarus insisted, were nonexistent, so Christ's alleged divinity was fallacious. The medical missionary and theologian Albert Schweitzer was to write a pathbreaking summary of eighteenth- and nineteenth-century interpretations of the gospel by several theologians and scholars. He regarded Reimarus as the originator of his era's fascination with the life of the historical Jesus.[7]

Schweitzer himself was skeptical about Christianity's traditional story of the life of Christ, but he was very sympathetic to the end-times preaching of Jesus, which was fulsomely covered by Reimarus. But even Schweitzer caught a whiff of the deep hostility and animosity of Reimarus to the orthodox Christian view. "Seldom," Schweitzer wrote, "has there been a hate so eloquent, so lofty a scorn; but then it is seldom that a work has been written in the just consciousness of so absolute a superiority of contemporary opinion."[8] What was becoming evident here was not just a skepticism about the veracity of the Bible but a deep rage against Jesus himself and his claims to authority and sovereignty. Many Americans were skeptical of the claims of Christians to know truth that had been revealed by God himself, but until the second half of the nineteenth century there was almost unanimous admiration for the virtues of Jesus himself. In Europe, that admiration had essentially died out among biblical critics and even theologians by the beginning of the nineteenth century, and particularly by the time of the death of Hegel in 1831.

The Romantic movement in literature, art, and music, which emphasized the supposed virtues of rebellion and personal egotism in contrast to the mass of society, certainly nourished this squabble with orthodox Christian belief. There was thus a coming together—not for the first time in history—of Romantic rage against life itself and a growing animosity toward traditional Christian doctrine. Few people epitomized this more succinctly than the English poet Percy Bysshe Shelley. From an early age, Shelley was fascinated by Promethean Romantic heroes, those who challenged the gods and expired in a flash of glory while pulling down the entire world around them. Shelley was also fascinated by the occult from a very early age. He achieved some notoriety at Oxford University as an undergraduate by being "sent down" (expelled) for printing at his own expense what at that time was believed to be the first printed atheist tract in English history, "The Necessity of Atheism."

In *Prometheus Unbound*, Shelley seemed to stumble on the concept of the historical outworking of the Hegelian dialectic. That outworking was apparently embodied in the function of a character in *Prometheus Unbound* called Demogorgon. As the critic Harold Bloom writes about Demogorgon,

> His only attributes are dialectical; he is the god of all those at the churning, at the reversing of cycles. Like the dialectic of the Marxists, Demogorgon is a necessitarian and materialistic entity, part of the nature of things as they are. But he represents the shadowy descent of the Holy Spirit in most dialectics of history, though it would be more accurate to call him a demonic parody of the Holy Spirit, just as the whole of *Prometheus Unbound* is a dark parody of the Christian salvation myth.[9]

"Necessitarian"? That is not a term most Americans understand at first glance. It in fact means an entity or person that believes absolutely everything is determined regardless both of personal volition and the normal chain of cause and effect. In other words, Shelley's creation was a rather unpleasant personality.

In the revolt against the Bible during the 1820s in Germany, one curious feature was the view held by some writers that the historicity of the Gospels and the details of the life of Christ were more or less irrelevant to real life. At least, such details were surely less important than the psychological and moral value of religiosity. This was the position of Friedrich Schleiermacher, who for a time exerted influence on the youthful Friedrich Engels, Karl Marx's collaborator. Schleiermacher wrote, among other things, "The Holy Books have become the Bible in virtue of their own power, but they do not forbid any other book from being or becoming a Bible in its turn."[10] In short, for Schleiermacher, whether the Bible was true or not was irrelevant. "Truth" itself was beginning to lose its power as a concept in Christian thought.

The moral and intellectual ambivalence of this view fit in perfectly with the moral and intellectual doubts and ambiguities of the views of the German philosophers who came after Hegel. Some of Hegel's followers and admirers wanted pretty much everything to remain as it had been when Hegel was alive: a strong Prussian state, excellent universities, and a thriving economy. But another group of young men—women did not play a visible role in German intellectual life at the time—soon became known as the Young Hegelians. They were much more radical in their worldview. In the Young Hegelian scheme of things, the end goal could be nothing less than the complete transformation of human society. This required a radical repudiation of Christian belief. Why? Because, in their view, Christianity stood in the way of the new and emerging Hegelian worldview and of the radical reordering of Prussian and indeed European life in accordance with that worldview. Germany was not yet a united empire and consisted of a patchwork of hereditary monarchies, principalities, and free cities. But it was in the Kingdom of Prussia, the most powerful of those monarchies, that the root of radical anti-Christian thought took root.

The first really important book that combined criticism of orthodox Christian belief with a positive philosophy of history along the lines suggested by Hegel was by the German scholar David Friedrich Strauss. His *The Life of Jesus, Critically Examined*, published in 1835, scandalized churchgoing Christians in Germany because it expressed flat disbelief in the major narrated incidents of the Gospels: it completely rejected the resurrection, calling it a "myth" invented by the disciples. It approached the life of Christ as illustrated in the Synoptic Gospels (Matthew, Mark, and Luke) in an idiosyncratic way: first by discounting any supernaturalist interpretation of Scripture, then from the perspective of a supernaturalist view of Christian orthodoxy, and then with the suggestion of a Hegelian synthesis between the two perspectives. The approach of Strauss was implicitly anti-miraculous, though he refused to take sides in his text.

The effect of reading *The Life of Jesus* for many contemporaries was devastating. One wrote, "It was Strauss's *The Life of Jesus* that filled both me and a number of my companions with Hegelian attitudes and also made us more and more disillusioned with theology. The spell that this book exercised over me was indescribable; I never read any book with so much pleasure and thoroughness. . . . It was as though scales fell from my eyes and a great light was shone on my path."[11]

Bruno Bauer was a Young Hegelian, a graduate student who had studied for three years under Hegel, and was associated with a group of like-minded graduate students called "The Doctors' Club" in Berlin. Karl Marx himself was invited to become a member in 1837. Bruno Bauer for a time had a great influence on Karl Marx. His vicious attacks on Christianity offended many, even in the intellectually sophisticated city of Berlin, and brought about his transfer from the University of Berlin to the University of Bonn. Bauer took Hegel's theory of history—that it was unfolding according to the principles of Hegel's *Geist* (spirit)—to its logical conclusion. If, as Hegel had written, history was an endlessly unfolding dialectical process, then Christianity must not be its highest product. The natural focus of Bauer's worldview was the idea of self-consciousness, the coming-to-adulthood, so to speak, of humans' ability to be aware of themselves and of life in general. Bauer had what even the mildly spoken Albert Schweitzer regarded as a "pathological" hatred of Christianity. Arnold Ruge, another Young Hegelian who was a central figure in the publication of views of the Young Hegelians of the late 1830s, dubbed Bauer "the Robespierre of theology."[12]

It was probably not an exaggeration. In retrospect, it is amazing that a professor of theology at a German university could be paid to spout venomous denunciations of orthodox Christian beliefs (well, perhaps not so amazing, given the current situation on United States college campuses). Bauer himself at one point described his actions as literally "demonic." In 1841 he wrote to Arnold Ruge: "I give lectures here at the university at the front of a large auditorium. I do not know myself when I pronounce my blasphemies on the podium; they are so enormous that they cause the students' hair to stand up, these little children to whom no one should give offense. And it sets me thinking how piously I work at home on my apology for Scripture and revelation. It is, in any event, a very wicked demon which grabs hold of me each time when I mount the podium, and I am so weak that I inevitably succumb to it."[13]

Hegel had theorized that the *Geist* sought to create human self-consciousness and self-awareness in the world through the activities of man. In other words, though the idea was miles away from anything authentically Christian, mankind, by obtaining true consciousness of itself, might end up thinking God's thoughts. But that idea was turned decisively on its head by the work of Ludwig Feuerbach. In his landmark book, *The Essence of Christianity*, Feuerbach over and over again made the point that God did not create religion, man did. In fact, God, in all his greatest imagined virtues, is basically man. Feuerbach was equally dismissive of Hegel's thought. He wrote: "Hegelian philosophy is the last, ambitious attempt to re-establish lost, defeated Christianity by means of philosophy, by following the universal modern procedure and identifying the negation of Christianity with Christianity itself."[14] Feuerbach, as the late Anglican bishop John Robinson noted in his influential work of the 1960s *Honest to God*, was not so much an atheist as an anti-theist; he wanted to *destroy* the idea of God because, Feuerbach believed, insofar as man worshiped an imaginary God, he was depriving himself of his true essence.[15]

The influence of Feuerbach's ideas on European thought was earthshaking. Friedrich Engels wrote about a powerful "impression of deliverance" felt by many young men, not just in Germany, after reading *The Essence of Christianity*. Engels wrote, "Then came Feuerbach's *Essence of Christianity*. With one blow it pulverized the contradiction, in that without circumlocutions it placed materialism on the throne again. . . . Enthusiasm was general: we all became at once Feuerbachians."[16] Indeed, Engels was not exaggerating. It is hard to think of a single major philosopher in the nineteenth century who was not converted to an anti-God mindset by Feuerbach. In 1844, Engels also wrote,

"The question has previously always been: what is God? And German philosophy has answered the question in this sense: God is man."[17]

In *The Essence of Christianity*, Feuerbach spelled out the realization that *man was actually God* as the turning point of history. He wrote, "The necessary turning-point of history is therefore the open confession, that the consciousness of God is nothing else than the consciousness of the species . . . that there is no other essence which man can think, dream of, imagine, feel, believe in, wish for, love and adore as the *absolute*, than the essence of human nature itself."[18]

Even before becoming part of the Young Hegelians, Karl Marx had been clawing his way up the ramparts of a visceral hatred of Christianity that was rooted in a sort of Romantic Prometheanism, a rage against all gods. Feuerbach helped him realize why Hegelian idealism was not the end point of his own philosophical journey. The culmination of Marx's search for precisely the right note in his critique of Christianity is to be found in one of his early writings that contains the famous quote, "Religion is the opium of the people." This is the thirteen-page article titled "Critique of Hegel's Philosophy of Law. Introduction." Marx writes:

> For Germany, the *criticism of religion* has been essentially completed, and the criticism is the prerequisite of all criticism. . . . Man, who has found only the *reflection* of himself in the fantastic reality of heaven, where he sought a superman, will no longer feel disposed to find the mere *appearance* of himself, the non-man, where he seeks and must seek his true reality. Religion is the sigh of the oppressed creature, the heart of a heartless world, and the soul of soulless conditions. It is the opium of the people.[19]

Well before the God-hating atheist had transformed himself into a brilliant theoretician with the goal of destroying capitalism, Marx himself had drunk "the German poison" with lasting and devastating consequences for the rest of humanity.

THE COLLAPSE OF AMERICA'S CHRISTIAN UNIVERSITIES

It is a remarkable historical fact that America's major universities went from being repositories of knowledge and teaching deeply imbued with the Christian worldview in the middle of the nineteenth century, with few exceptions, to uniformly antireligious and specifically anti-Christian institutions by the end of the twentieth century. As the Second Great Awakening wound down by the 1850s, American universities still bore the firm imprint of the mostly Congregational-style Christian culture of New England. In 1840, four-fifths of the college presidents of denominationally related colleges were clergymen, as were two-thirds of state college presidents. Faculty members were accustomed to being expected to keep a close eye on the students, just as their parents would.[20] Yet by 2007, Ontario Consultants on Religious Tolerance was reporting a survey that showed an incredible 53 percent of college faculty at two-year and four-year colleges in the United States had unfavorable attitudes towards evangelical Christians.[21] On many college campuses, some teaching departments pushed hard to eliminate any trace of Christian presence on the territory of the college.

There were many reasons for this radical alteration of the worldview of the academy in general toward the Christian faith, and in this section we will deal with some of the more prominent factors: the importation into American college life of the ideas of intellectual skepticism that had dominated German philosophy and much of academic life since the 1830s; the transformation of American colleges and universities themselves into institutions focusing largely on science and research, the advent of Darwinism, and the ascendancy of the ideas of positivist philosophy; the emergence of articulate and self-confident agnostics and religious skeptics in American society; and finally—and perhaps most important—the devastating impact on attitudes of moral self-restraint introduced into American life by the social and cultural revolution of the 1960s.

A respected historian of the emergence of the modern American university has put it well. "To overstate the case only slightly," George Marsden writes in *The Soul of the American University*, "in New England the college was the parent of the colony. The New England experiment was largely the product of an old-boy network of Emmanuel [College, Cambridge] graduates, including John Harvard himself, with their close Puritan allies from a number of other colleges. When the founders decided to settle their college in Newtown, the new name they chose for the town was Cambridge."[22] Yet higher education in New England was integrated into the entirety of social policy.

Harvard, for example, was founded in 1636 for the express purpose of training clergy. About half the Harvard graduates of the seventeenth century became clergy, and in fact the regulations of Harvard College in 1646, ten years after its founding, stated that every student (there were no women admitted at the time), "shall consider the main End of his life and studies, to know God and Jesus Christ which is Eternal life."[23] Indeed, from the mid-seventeenth to the mid-eighteenth century, Harvard and Yale constituted virtually the whole of higher education in America.

It is a curious fact, however, that within a century of Harvard's founding for the training of Congregational clergy, the faculty of Yale was distinctly hostile to the preaching of the most outstanding evangelist of the First Great Awakening, George Whitefield. In 1744, the Harvard faculty actually characterized Whitefield as an "uncharitable, censorious and slanderous Man" and, worst of all, an "Enthusiast" (meaning that he claimed direct guidance from the Spirit of God). The term "Enthusiast," in fact, as applied to evangelicals in the First Great Awakening and the Wesleyan revival in England, carried exactly the same derogatory connotation as does the word "Fundamentalist" in the twenty-first century when applied to contemporary evangelicals: uncouth, probably uneducated, and filled with zeal for the spiritual progress of other people.

With the triumph of the American revolution and the political coalition of Deists, liberals, and Baptists who supported Thomas Jefferson for president—not to mention the prominence of Thomas Paine, author of *Common Sense* in 1776 and *The Age of Reason* in 1793—the intellectual atmosphere at both Harvard and Yale became more open to Free Thought and to ideas of learning not as narrowly Calvinistic in content as several decades earlier. There was a basic philosophical commitment to the fundamental moral assumptions of Protestantism, but the doctrinal core of early New England theology, the Calvinist belief that mankind was fallen and needed Christ alone for its rescue, had been eclipsed by a "common sense theology," a philosophy brought over from Scotland by the theologian and educator John Witherspoon. The common sense philosophy held that the principles of good human morality could be inferred from nature and that they affirmed the Christian moral outlook and indeed the truth of Christian revelation. Common sense philosophy also held that science and the fundamental teachings of Christian revelation were in accord with each other. Two texts widely read and taught in American colleges in the decades after the American Revolution were Joseph Butler's *The Analogy of Religion, Natural and Revealed* (1736) and William Paley's immensely influential *Natural Theology* (1802).[24]

At least until the 1820s, common sense philosophy held sway over American thought. William Paley's book was broadly accepted by most Christians as the best expression available of the argument by design for God's role in the creation of the world and of nature. The argument by design of theists, then and now, holds that nature itself is so inherently sophisticated in its workings that it must have been designed by someone outside of itself. Paley's famous argument was that if a person unfamiliar with a watch came across a watch on his or her morning walk, he or she would assume automatically from its complicated mechanisms that someone had designed it. Thus today, say theists, the world we live is so much more complex and beautiful than a watch that it seems to give us clear evidence of a Creator infinitely greater than the creation.

On the basis of the Scottish common sense philosophy, there was also an assumption that the findings of scientific observation would confirm the Christian message. Marsden and others, however, have argued that the very monolithic and homogeneous nature of American Protestantism "eventually contributed to the virtual exclusion of religious perspective from the most influential centers of American intellectual life."[25] Marsden claims that this took place because, for the sake of participating in a broad American philosophical consensus of the virtues of democracy and the "natural" reasonableness of traditional Christian morality, American Protestants in higher education left themselves vulnerable to movements within natural philosophy that eventually would turn against Christianity in general.

Ironically, this vulnerability became apparent with the growth of the American public school movement, the continuing American geographic expansion out west, and the increasingly accepted view that the best foundation for good public education should be a sort of generic Christianity that is not only disestablished in an organizational way from the churches but also disentangled from the theological beliefs that had originally given rise to it. In Massachusetts, for example, Horace Mann, secretary of the state board of education from 1837 to 1848, emphasized Bible reading in the public schools and the inculcation of the precepts of Christianity. Mann had actually been raised as a Calvinist but then became a Unitarian and regarded a Calvinist education as an "unspeakable calamity." While some critics argued that Mann was in fact establishing in education an irreligion (a charge previously leveled against Thomas Jefferson), his persistent support for the value of the Bible and Christian morality made it difficult for these arguments to gain much traction.[26] Another factor ensuring continuing support for Horace Mann's mission in American education was a widespread suspicion of Roman Catholicism among American Protestants. Horace Bushnell's *Christian Nurture* (1847) argued, "We are still, as Americans, a Protestant people."[27]

That sentiment was reinforced by the increasing number of American students who were studying in Germany. Most of them were studying at the University of Berlin, a resolutely Protestant institution. The University of Berlin had been founded in 1810 by the Kingdom of Prussia, and in the century between 1815 and 1914, an estimated ten thousand American students went to Germany to study. George Marsden estimates that in the decades leading up to 1850, a period when hundreds of new American colleges were being founded, as many as a quarter of all Americans who went abroad to study went to Germany.[28]

Some of them may indeed have imbibed the waters of D. F. Strauss, Bruno Bauer, and Feuerbach, but even those who didn't couldn't have been unaware of the idealist thinking of men like Johann Gottlieb Fichte, whose emphasis on the philosophy of self-consciousness was still powerful. Fichte wrote, "The true end of Learning, the genuine fruit of knowledge is the development of the human soul that it may become wise, pure, and—that it may reach that perfection which is the ultimate ground of its existence."[29] An American admirer of German idealist philosophy was Henry Tappan, who was elected the first president of the University of Michigan. Described by some as the "John the Baptist of the American university," Tappan held a concept of the university as an institution with a wide degree of academic freedom, a talented faculty at its heart, and academic professionalism. Of university professors, Tappan wrote, "However amiable his character, however pure his religious or political creed according to the judgment of any sect of party, if he have not the requisite literary of scientific qualifications, he is of no account."[30]

Tappan accomplished much at Michigan, though he was ultimately relieved of his position by the regents of the university, who found him egotistical. Tappan was broadly evangelical Christian in his worldview, and he supported daily chapel for the students. He alienated some, however, by serving wine at dinner in his own home and by permitting Michigan students to drink beer. At a time when the temperance movement among American evangelicals was already strong, this did not go down very well among the mainly Republican regents.

But with the Northern victory in the American Civil War and the rapid growth of industry, business, and indeed personal fortunes in the North, American university education began to experience a historic upheaval. In the first half of the nineteenth century, as we have seen, a majority of American colleges had Christian denominational connections, and their presidents and other senior faculty and administrators were largely drawn from ordained clergy. An increasingly large and influential body of university reformers of more liberal theological viewpoint resented the evangelical shadow that they thought hung over American higher education.

An additional factor in the changes in American universities was the perception that, like the great German universities at which so many Americans had studied, universities ought to be places of learning where the emphasis was on research. By contrast, most American colleges had traditionally functioned as institutions with the goal of transforming inexperienced and sometimes shy youths into mature adults. American colleges were expected to function, in large measure, as behaving in loco parentis toward students. With the evolution of large private and state universities that stressed the training of serious, research-orientated graduate students, the *in loco parentis* role of universities tended to atrophy.

The president of Brown University, Francis Wayland, was a graduate of Andover Theological Seminary who saw no contradiction between science and religion, and he thought that all scientific discoveries would ultimately lead people back to belief in a Creator. But Wayland was also pragmatic and a strong believer in the value of industrial progress and the need for technology to serve the nation. "Nothing," Wayland wrote, "would tend so much to the progress of wealth among us as the diffusion throughout the whole people of a knowledge of the principles of science, and the application of science to the arts."[31]

Wayland was attentive to the fact that economic prosperity produced great fortunes, and he was also aware of the effect that great fortunes could have on American university education as a whole. John D. Rockefeller's massive fortune was employed to bolster—if not jump-start—the University of Chicago. In a possibly more far-reaching alliance of wealth and academic idealism, New York state financier Ezra Cornell deployed his fortune to founding Cornell University under the administrative leadership of Andrew Dickson White. It was Henry Tappan who had first noticed White and brought him to teach at the University of Michigan. White was a liberal Episcopalian and was yet another American who had imbibed the heady waters of "the German poison" at the University of Berlin.

Whatever else White acquired in Berlin, his experience there strengthened his antipathy toward any version of Christian "sectarianism." In fact, at the time of the opening of Cornell in 1868, opponents of the university who wanted state education funds for their own institutions dubbed it "godless."[32] White immediately responded: "We will labor to make this a Christian institution—a sectarian institution it will never be."[33] White was nominally an Episcopalian, though he had never been confirmed. But when he hired Felix Adler, a secular Jew, to teach students in 1874, he ran into trouble. Adler had founded the Ethical Culture Society in 1876, and at Cornell some of his courses openly attacked religion; his contract was not renewed in 1877.

In fact, 1877 proved an important year for the role of the Christian faith in American universities and colleges. The prevailing Christian consensus at universities where scientific research was encouraged held that all truth, if investigated and arrived at through honest research, would sooner or later confirm the claims of Christianity. "Nineteenth century Americans," writes Julie Reuben, "were confident that natural science supported Christianity. 'If God is,' wrote Harvard philosopher Andrew P. Peabody, 'he must have put his signature on his whole creation no less than his impress on his manifested or written world. The hieroglyphs of nature must needs correspond to the alphabetic writing of revelation.'"[34] This, of course, was a classic statement of the argument of "design" as an explanation of the way nature is.

The difficulty was that, after the Civil War, more and more Americans were persuaded that science and revealed religion were in a sort of mortal conflict and that science would ultimately prevail. Darwinism had arrived at American colleges and universities by the 1860s, and at first there was little organized opposition to it; many clergy believed that evolution was one of the truths of science that would eventually confirm Christianity. But a major sea change started to take place in the 1870s. The decade was marked by the beginning of what historian of Free Thought Susan Jacoby considers the high-water mark of Free Thought as an influential movement in American society.[35]

Some of the changes at American universities involved huge shifts in the orientation of learning and teaching as what had previously been denominational Christian colleges shrugged off their Christian organizational ties and headed out into the hitherto unknown horizons of university education in which science was the sole concept generally agreed upon as good for the human race. Science as a concept, moreover, was no longer viewed as a definite ally of Christian faith.

After 1877, big changes occurred at universities. As Julie Reuben points out in her excellent history of the rise of the modern

American university, in the decade after the 1870s, "reform-oriented schools discontinued lectures on natural theology and evidences of Christianity. The University of California offered its last class in natural theology in 1871. At Harvard, Professor Andrew P. Peabody in 1872 stopped assigning a text on the 'evidences of Christianity' in his moral philosophy course." The only exception to this trend was Yale, at the time the most philosophically and theologically conservative of major American education institutions. The president of Yale in the 1880s, Noah Porter, still required his students in the 1880s to take a class called "Natural Theology and Evidences of Christianity."[36]

The trend both in academic courses at other universities and in society as a whole was moving against Christian thought as the preferred worldview of higher education. For one thing, Darwin's theory that the forces of nature would decide among themselves which species survived and flourished and which vanished from the scene was given a boost by sociologist and historian Herbert Spencer, who coined the term "survival of the fittest" (it was *not* Darwin's phrase). This concept had two consequences, one of them limited to its time period and one of them with disastrous consequences for America and humanity as a whole.

"Survival of the fittest" was a flattering notion for the newly emerging batch of successful capitalists, including some of the more rapacious of the ultra-rich in the decades of the 1880s and 1890s. It suggested that the dog-eat-dog worldview that some of them exhibited was entirely underwritten by the scientific discoveries and conclusions of Darwinism. One disastrous outcome of the broad diffusion of the notion of "survival of the fittest" was the emergence of supposedly "scientific" ideas about nation, race, and culture. In Germany, the idea of the superiority of German civilization as a result of Darwinian selection took root even before World War I, but its most deleterious consequences occurred when it was adopted by Hitler and the Nazis before and during World War II.

But even before Adolf Hitler came to power in Germany, one of the most energetic supporters of the idea of "the survival of the fittest" was Margaret Sanger, the founder of Planned Parenthood. Sanger wrote a famous book in 1922, *The Pivot of Civilization*, that enthusiastically advocates redressing "the lack of balance between the birthrate of the 'fit' and the 'unfit.'" And who are "the unfit"? "The feeble-minded, the mentally defective, and the poverty-stricken." According to Sanger, the mentally defective bred at a prodigiously faster rate than "the fit," and society, therefore, should enforce limits to their fertility. Birth control for Sanger was "the greatest and truly eugenic method" for improving the human race.[37] Darwin himself, of course, favored the view that some parts of the human race were breeding too fast for the good of the rest of it. In *The Descent of Man*, he had warned everyone against the danger of "the careless, the squalid, unaspiring Irishman [who] multiplies like rabbits," whereas the "frugal, foreseeing, self-respecting Scot, stern in morality, spiritual in his faith, sagacious and disciplined in his intelligence, passes his best years in struggle and in celibacy, marries late, and leaves few behind him."[38] Of course, Darwin failed to note that if the Scot was indeed "spiritual in his faith," it had not come about through natural selection, but more likely through the "sagacious" Christian evangelism of John Knox and many others.

Sanger, like most zealous exponents of Darwin's ideas, was an atheist and was adamantly opposed to what she called "the debauch of sentimentalism" or "the cruelty of charity." Christian charity, of course, operates on the belief that all human beings are made in the image of God and are worthy of respect and dignity, but Sanger would have none of this. "Charity," she said, "encourages the healthier and more normal sections of the world to shoulder the burden of unthinking and indiscriminate fecundity of others; which brings with it, as I think the reader must agree, the dead weight of stocks that are more detrimental to the future of the race and the world, it tends to render them to a menacing degree dominant."[39]

Sanger, of course, had not at this point developed her ideas on eugenics, which even Planned Parenthood, on its official website, regards as "objectionable and outmoded." Many thoughtful Christian leaders of American colleges and universities, however, were worried that the trend toward theological liberalism and even agnosticism in society as a whole would be detrimental to the preservation of Christian conviction in academic life. In 1879, Noah Porter, the president of Yale, attempted to stop a Yale professor, William Graham Sumner, from using Herbert Spencer's *The Study of Sociology* as a textbook in his courses. Sumner, in fact, was Rev. Graham Sumner, an able if somewhat authoritarian teacher who had been ordained as an Episcopal priest. What seems to have happened is that, after his exposure to Darwin and Spencer, Sumner was converted to scientific naturalism through exposure to the ideas of these two thinkers and to those of T. H. Huxley, the man who in England had the reputation of "Darwin's bulldog." Sumner even ceased using the title "Reverend." As he explained later, "I never consciously gave up a religious belief. It was as if I had put my beliefs into a drawer, and when I opened it, there was nothing there at all."[40]

With Yale still being something of an old boys' club in 1880, Porter neither fired Sumner nor asked him to resign. In fact, he interceded with the Yale board, which, having read about the Porter-Sumner controversy in the *New York Times*, didn't like what it had read and wanted to authorize Porter to assert authority over the texts being used in the college. Sumner didn't resign but was kept on to continue to teach sociology into the twentieth century. Porter's objection to Spencer was that Sumner, through Spencer, was not only subscribing to a new worldview of scientific naturalism but also denying the possibility of the existence of any absolute. Spencer, in Porter's view, "excluded any absolute and asserted that observable phenomena are all we can know about."[41]

But in the debate emerging at the time over the authority of science over other social phenomena like religious belief, the new champion on the side of those trying to push Christianity out of American higher education was the philosophy of "logical positivism." This system had been developed by the French sociologist August Comte, who held that science must, to be true to its own principles, exclude religious considerations. There had been three broad ages in the development of science, according to Comte: the theological or fictional; the abstract or metaphysical; and the scientific or "positive." Logical positivists sharply distinguished between statements of knowledge and value judgments. Yet Comte himself, despite his expressions of misgiving about religion, devised his own religion of humanity to replace all existing religious systems.

While all this was going on at Yale, a major new spokesman for the freethinking or agnostic worldview was emerging in the form of Robert Green Ingersoll. In its reporting about the Sumner-Porter controversy at Yale, the *New York Times* had referred to Herbert Spencer as "the white czar of agnosticism," but that title more properly belonged to the skillful public speaker and debater Ingersoll, who was convinced that Darwin had destroyed the credibility of Christianity. "Write the name of Charles Darwin on the one hand and the name of every theologian who ever lived on the other, and from that name has come more light to the world than from all of those [theologians]. His doctrine of evolution, his doctrine of the survival of the fittest, his doctrine of the origin of species, has removed in every thinking mind the last vestige of orthodox Christianity."[42] In fact, evolutionary theory appealed to many Americans as the country flexed its vast industrial muscles in the last quarter of the nineteenth century and the population of the United States nearly doubled, from 38 million in 1870 to more than 70 million in 1900. Americans were optimistic about progress, and the era was one that stressed the success of the diligent individual.

At some of America's newer universities, the appeal of Darwinism had some interesting expressions among college professors and administrators who otherwise appeared to subscribe to the generic model of Christian morality, but in a nonsectarian way. David Starr Jordan, for example, was brought over to be the first president of Stanford University by Leland and Jane Stanford, the founding benefactors of the university, after serving as president of Indiana University. Jordan described himself as a "Puritan moralist," and he championed high ideals of public and personal morality.[43] Jordan, however, did not seem to believe that science would confirm the beliefs of traditional Christianity. "To say that the university is scientific is to say that it is genuine, that it is devoted to realities, not to make-believes and shams."[44]

Jordan, however, went well beyond a mere championship of science against "make-believes and shams." Science, for him, conceived of Jesus Christ as the ultimate goal of evolution itself.

Religion in general, Jordan thought, would itself evolve in a way not unlike Japanese Shintoism, which, he said, "has no creed, no ceremonies necessary to its practice . . . no sacred legend of mystery, and nothing of the machinery of spiritual power which characterizes great religions on other countries."[45]

The founding president of Cornell University, Andrew Dickson White, another Episcopalian clergyman who strongly resented not just sectarianism in general but evangelicals in particular, spent much of his scholarly life working on a major opus that was finally published in 1896, *A History of the Warfare of Science with Theology in Christendom*. Originally, White had intended to give the impression that his beef was with the specialized and sometimes esoteric field of Christian theology, but by the time of the book's publication, he was quite open about his objective: "a frontal attack on all traditional Christian and biblical belief." Citing Darwinism, he said that "the old theory of direct creation is gone forever" and that creation stories were part of the evolution of humanity.[46] As Marsden described White's bombshell, "White proceeded to furnish a complete handbook for turn-of-the-century skepticism regarding traditional Christianity, his assault culminating in exposition of the incredibility of biblical accounts of miracles, the superiority of modern medicine and psychology over biblicist supernatural explanations, and of how Higher Criticism [criticism of the veracity of the Bible by biblical scholars] had altogether demolished biblical credibility in scientific and historical matters."[47]

By now, however, the tide had turned decisively in his favor, and White felt free to launch his attack. He argued, as we have seen, that "the old theory of direct creation is gone forever" and that "we now understand the creation stories themselves as products of the evolution of humanity." White later wrote,

"I believed then, and am convinced now, that it was a struggle between Science and Dogmatic Theology. More and more, I saw that it was a conflict between two epochs in the evolution of human thought—the theological and the scientific."[48]

At Princeton Theological Seminary, Professor Charles Hodge in 1873 had a blunt answer to the question that titled his own article: "What Is Darwinism?" He had the following simple response: "Darwinism is atheism." Hodge was not an uneducated or illiterate clergyman but one who believed solidly in natural development of different species. But he saw in Darwinism a theory of a universe that made sense to him. Over time, he held, it was possible for blind, random causation to create intelligence from non-intelligence.[49]

As science increasingly assumed the role of ultimate authority in higher education, its champions began describing its function in quasi-religious terms. Proponents of science described themselves as "priests" guarding the "temple" of science and students of science as "worshipers." At the same time, Germany's notion of biblical higher criticism—that is, criticism of the Bible that sought to understand the meaning of the text in its historical context—had finally made its way across the Atlantic, ravaging the quiet acceptance of the authority of Scripture that had characterized the Second Great Awakening and that had, until the final quarter of the nineteenth century, protected American universities from full-scale and outright apostasy from Christian belief.

Not all the critics and opponents of Christianity were of one mind in their views. The educational philosopher and psychologist John Dewey, for example, regarded as one of the founders of the American philosophical school of pragmatism, was opposed to the idea of agnosticism, the very term that Ingersoll embraced in his atheism. Dewey regarded agnosticism as an unstable "compromise . . . a treaty of partition which would divide the kingdom of reality into halves, and proclaim one supernatural and unknowable, the other natural and the realm of knowledge."[50] Dewey, however, was already developing the view that became associated with him, namely that "education is the fundamental method of social progress and reform . . . the community's duty to education is, therefore, its paramount moral duty."[51] Dewey's ideas were enormously influential on educational ideas both in the United States and overseas. In 1908, Dewey and his former colleague at the University of Chicago, James H. Tufts, published *Ethics*. Within a month of its appearance, thirty American colleges and universities had selected it as the textbook of choice for courses on ethics. There were, in fact, twenty-five separate printings of *Ethics* until it was substantially revised in 1932. Dewey and Tufts both rejected supernatural origins of ethics and presented the phenomenon as a natural development from social life.

In addition, a whole new field of study at America's universities was pushing Christianity out of the back door of university life. This was the "scientific" study of comparative religion. Though most scholars were generally sympathetic to religion as a beneficial ingredient of all human society, they were increasingly of the view that religion had no significant intellectual content; that its function in human society was, at best, of utilitarian value; and that it needed to be examined detachedly, like, say, any species of butterfly. As we have seen, some university scholars were suggesting that there might be a religion of the future, with belief content as yet unknown. When Charles Eliot, the president of Harvard, gave a speech in 1909 just before his retirement, he actually championed a "Religion of the Future" as an alternative to traditional Christianity.

The worlds of anthropology and religion were also profoundly shaken up by books like *The Golden Bough* by Sir James Frazer. Frazer, an anthropologist who was for a long time considered to be the father of modern anthropology, suggested that all religions in all cultures share core beliefs indigenous to the religious legacy of the entire human race. These included, but were not limited to, fertility cults and the belief that a sacred king needed to sacrifice himself for the good of his community. It was a long way from the statement of Christian faith originally required as a matriculating standard for any student to wishing to enroll at Harvard College.

There was a strong consensus at universities that the comparative study of religion would provide great insights into understanding, and indeed improving, human social behavior. At the same time, the commitment of universities to religious freedom made it difficult for professors to prescribe what the religious preference of students should be. This led to an almost comical situation at Johns Hopkins University in 1918 when students had to petition the board of trustees to allow evangelist Billy Sunday to speak on campus.

Between about 1910 and 1930, Sunday was America's best-known evangelist. Until the appearance of evangelist Billy Graham in the 1950s, Sunday had preached in person to more people than any other American. He was also a broadly popular person, ranking number eight in a list of "the greatest men in America" and an occasional guest at the White House. Despite their grudging respect for religious freedom, the faculty of Johns Hopkins, which was to a significant degree agnostic or quite liberal in its Christian theology, was strongly against Sunday's visit. Philosophy professor Arthur O. Lovejoy spoke for many of them when he told the trustees, "Billy Sunday is a man who, whatever his usefulness in dealing with certain classes of people, represents, both in his intellectual temper and his taste, an attitude which should be antipodal to that of any body of university men."[52] Put another way, Lovejoy was content to let Sunday speak to the unwashed American masses, but not to the cream of America's emerging academic elite at major universities.

Lovejoy's attitude represented a failure of universities in general to integrate religion into the intellectual life of the university. America's university reformers, after all, had wanted to reform American universities partly to avoid the "sectarianism" that they thought would be the price that learning would have to pay for any denominational connection, and also in order to import the German system of academic freedom, faculty authority, and strong specialization of learning and research. But, as historian Julie Reuben sums up the dilemma, this stance by the university reformers and their "adherence to scientific standards of inquiry precluded a strong religious presence in higher education."[53]

The tendency of American university campuses to adopt a naturalistic worldview that was dubious about Christianity's supernaturalism claims was firmly in place by the 1920s. A study of significant scientists in 1916—including, of course, many in senior positions on university campuses—by Bryn Mawr psychologist James Leuba uncovered the fact that about 45.5 percent said they believed in a personal God, about the same number disbelieved, and the remainder had no opinion.[54] (A study asking identical questions in 1996 showed a slight increase in the number of convinced atheists—45 percent—but exactly the same percentage of theists. Leuba had predicted that over a period of time, there would be a significant reduction in the number of theists among scientists.)[55] He summed up his findings: "The essential problem facing organized Christianity is constituted by the wide-spread rejection of its two fundamental dogmas—a rejection apparently destined to extend parallel with the diffusion of knowledge and the intellectual and moral qualities that make for eminence in scholarly pursuits."[56] Leuba's prediction that Christian belief would dwindle on college campuses had held true: today on American university campuses Christian believers are a distinct, and sometimes tiny, minority. That has been true for probably nearly a century.

The climax of American mockery of Christian belief, at least in the larger public setting, was the famous Scopes trial of 1925 in Dayton, Tennessee. The trial was held to try a Dayton schoolteacher, John Scopes, on charges that he had violated the Butler Act, a Tennessee statute recently passed that made the teaching of Darwinian evolution illegal in the state. Scopes was defended by the agnostic Chicago attorney Clarence Darrow, who had in turn been contacted by the American Civil Liberties Union. The public mood of mockery toward the people of Dayton and Christian antievolutionists was relentless and cruel, and special spice was added by the acidulous pen of H. L. Mencken, a columnist for the *Baltimore Sun*. Mencken supported eugenics as well as social Darwinism, and he bore an unmistakable contempt for people of strong Christian conviction, especially if they came from the South.

It was not only cynical intellectuals like H. L. Mencken, however, who contributed to the public ridiculing of belief in creation and a Creator God. The Scopes trial generated a series of dramatic reenactments of the trial's inherent drama, the most famous and popular of which was first the play and then the movie *Inherit the Wind*. The plot of both the play and the movie pivots around a thinly disguised fictional town of Hillsboro (i.e., Dayton), agnostic lawyer Henry Drummond (Clarence

Darrow), and a fundamentalist politician named Matthew Henry Bradley (William Jennings Bryan). Even Scopes himself, in an autobiography published many years later, acknowledged that the screenplay took "liberties" with the actual story, including inventing a preposterous romance between Scopes and a preacher's daughter and containing a scene with the protagonist Cates (i.e., Scopes) sitting in jail. Scopes, of course, was not only never arrested, he was never even summoned as a witness in the trial, mainly because Darrow and his defense team could not factually establish that Scopes had ever taught biology and thus even mentioned the term evolution. Hollywood had its fun, and *Inherit the Wind* was enduringly popular. But as noted by Ronald A. Numbers, a historian of Darwinism's arrival in the United States and himself a supporter of Darwinism, the movie "grossly caricatures the stated opinions of the protagonists." Numbers specifically criticizes the historians who drafted the *National Standards for United States History* for recommending the movie as a key to understanding Bryan's "fundamentalist thinking." He writes: "That strikes me as a little like recommending *Gone with the Wind* as a historically reliable account of the Civil War."[57]

Darwinism, of course, had already won the battle in the American academy, if not at the popular level, as a coup de grace against the truth-claim assertions of Christianity. But a far more important factor is that entirely non-Christian conceptions of human behavior, especially sexual behavior, had by the end of the 1920s triumphed broadly in public life and entertainment in America: namely the ideas of Austrian-born psychiatrist Sigmund Freud. Freud almost single-handedly developed an entire vocabulary of human behavior that has permeated Western culture—ideas like the superego, the ego, and the id float around in people's minds whether or not they have ever heard of Freud, much less read his work. It is hard even today to discuss human behavior without employing Freudian concepts about psychology, even though Freud's specific ideas about the superego, the ego, and the id largely have been abandoned by mainstream psychiatry. Nevertheless, "It is fair to say," Alister McGrath writes, "that from about 1920 Freud's account of religion gained the ascendancy within the American intelligentsia, attracting a following exceeding that of any other modernist or postmodernist thinker. Freud set the cultural agenda of his day and for a generation beyond in a way that justifies W. H. Auden's descriptions of him as 'not a person, but a whole climate of opinion.'"[58] Freud came into his own as an influence upon American culture in a decade, the 1920s, that almost certainly disrupted the course of American Christianity and traditional, Christian-based morality more profoundly than any previous decade in American history and until the revolutionary 1960s.

In terms of America's Christian churches, most of the older, mainline denominations—the Episcopalians, Presbyterians, and Methodists—experienced a decline in numbers during the 1930s. However, more evangelical groups, like Pentecostals and Baptists, actually grew. The Southern Baptist convention grew from four million at the beginning of the 1930s to five million by the end of it. Meanwhile, the fastest-growing institution of higher learning during the Depression during the early 1930s was the evangelical Christian university Wheaton College, in the suburbs of Chicago. An expression of the fundamentalists' revolt against the increasingly secular pattern of higher education in the United States was the establishment of Bob Jones University in Greenville, South Carolina, in 1927. Though his experience there was unhappy, the future American evangelist

Billy Graham enrolled briefly at Bob Jones University in the fall of 1936.

In retrospect, the Great Depression and the decade of the 1930s have been seen by some as a character-forming period in American life. *The Greatest Generation* was the title of a bestselling book by NBC television journalist Tom Brokaw in 1994.[59] Brokaw thought this generation, which came of age during the 1930s, was patriotic, courageous in World War II, and diligent in working and building families after the war ended. It was not, however, strikingly religious. In some respects, while the 1920s was a decade that mocked American Christianity, the following decade, preoccupied with recovering from economic catastrophe, all but ignored it.

But the soldiers being demobilized at the end of World War II were more than just courageous in combat and diligent at seeking jobs and building up families in peacetime: they were also spiritually questing. The beginning of the Cold War—in 1946, if it is reckoned as starting with Winston Churchill's Cold War speech at Fulton, Missouri—suddenly introduced Americans to the idea that massive destruction to themselves and American society could come very quickly and without warning. This understanding of the fragility of society and life itself led to one of the greatest Christian resurgences in American history, what Marvin Olasky has called the "fifth wind" of American Christian revival.

If this sudden new flourishing can be identified with any one individual, there is no question that it is the evangelist Billy Graham. At the end of World War II, Graham was invited to speak in the United States and in Europe to audiences of young people by Torrey Johnson, the founder of Youth for Christ. One of Graham's close friends at the time was fellow evangelist

Charles Templeton, a Canadian who was an eloquent speaker but who gradually lost his faith under the liberal teachings at Princeton Theological Seminary and who ultimately drifted into atheism.[60]

Graham's influence on American Christianity had its origins in the Greater Los Angeles Crusade of 1949. Among other Americans converted there was the World War II hero and former prisoner of war of the Japanese, Louis Zamperini, who had first come to fame after participating in the 1936 Olympics in Berlin and meeting Adolf Hitler. During World War II, Zamperini had crash-landed in the Pacific and survived a grim, forty-seven-day struggle for survival before being picked up by the Japanese navy. Zamperini was cruelly tortured as a POW in Japan, and on his return to the United States he was so embittered by his experience that he became an alcoholic. Graham's message of Christian salvation and forgiveness changed Zamperini's life and enabled him to become an effective motivational speaker.[61]

The stunning success of the Los Angeles crusade caused it to be extended to eight weeks instead of the originally scheduled three and propelled Graham into national attention in the United States. He was besieged by reporters from the Hearst organization and *Time* and *Life* magazines, whose founder and proprietor Henry Luce was struck by his dynamism. Graham instantly became a national icon. His evangelistic meetings were called "crusades," and throughout the 1950s and 1960s they were held in major cities throughout the United States. At the end of each evangelistic sermon, Graham would invite "inquirers" to leave their seats in the stadium where the crusade was being held and to "come forward" into an area in front of the podium, where they could be counseled by advisers specially trained for follow-up. The advisors would then direct the inquirers—essentially new converts to the evangelical version of Christianity—to churches in the city where the crusade was being held for further teaching and inclusion in the Christian community.

During the long and active portion of his career, both in the United States and overseas, Graham preached the gospel in person to more people (210 million in 185 countries) than any other individual in history. While by no means did all the "inquirers" at Billy Graham crusades turn into mature Christians, many did, and many of them developed in later life into prominent evangelists and Bible teachers. The Graham crusades certainly fueled a perception that Christianity was beginning a new growth spurt in the 1950s. This perception was enhanced by the prevailing belief in the White House and Congress during the 1950s that America's Christian roots should be made more prominent. The words "In God We Trust" officially became the United States' national motto and were gradually introduced into American coinage during the 1950s. The phrase "under God" was incorporated in the Pledge of Allegiance in 1954. President Eisenhower, who had never been known as a religious man throughout his military career, responded warmly to Graham when the two men met for the first time at the beginning of 1952, just before Eisenhower was inaugurated as president. "I think one of the reasons I was elected," Eisenhower told Graham, "was to help lead this country spiritually. We *need* a spiritual renewal."[62] Eisenhower also said (perhaps less helpfully from Graham's point of view), "There can be no good government without religion, and I don't care what religion it is."[63]

In retrospect, it has become a conventional viewpoint that the 1950s were a time of boring conformity in American life, of unimaginative adherence to bourgeois values that had originated, of course, somewhere back in America's once-Christian past. The 1950s were, in comparison to the decade that followed, socially conventional and predictable—with the obvious and important exception of the African-American campaign for civil rights, a campaign correctly linked to outspoken black Rev. Martin Luther King Jr. The decade, however, was also marked by the emergence of the "beat generation," an inchoate gathering of poets, artists, and writers who reveled in nonconformity and rejection of the moral and ethical standards of most of society. Exemplified in the lives of Allen Ginsburg, William S. Burroughs, Jack Kerouac, and others, the beats modeled a lifestyle of rejecting the traditional, the conventional, and above all the moral. Burroughs led a depraved life that involved extensive drug use and sexual activity with men, women, and children. The beats rejected anything that most Americans deemed honorable or worthy and, almost without being aware of it, lent to American culture a phenomenon of sloppy dress and unhygienic bodily appearance captured in the word *beatnik*. By the time of the late 1960s, *beatnik*, while not losing any of its characteristics, had been replaced by the word *hippie*. In essence, the "beat" lifestyle was inherently rebellious against the disciplined personal behavior that America's Christians had always assumed to be the godly ideal.

The beat movement was not a large-scale manifestation, but its main features were to erupt into prominence in America once the sixties were underway. As Roger Kimball writes of the beats, "Their programmatic anti-Americanism, their avid celebration of drug abuse, their squalid, promiscuous sex lives, their pseudo-spirituality, their attack on rationality and their degradation of intellectual standards, their aggressive narcissism and juvenile political posturing; in all this and more, the Beats were every bit as 'advanced' as any sixties radical."[64] Yet for all the continuities between the beats in the 1950s and the radicals of the 1960s, it was the sixties that eroded more decisively than any other period in American history the influence and respect of Christianity among Americans.

The 1960s, in objective terms, was a decade characterized by an unpopular American war in Southeast Asia, by the struggles of black Americans to achieve civil rights equality with white Americans, by a widespread revolution in sexual mores, and by interest in Eastern religions, to name but a few of the most prominent features. But the decade was also the beginning of a cultural revolution in American life that in many respects is still continuing. The sixties initiated, among other things, an ideology of radical egalitarianism mixed with hedonistic individualism. The odd-couple marriage of these two sometimes mutually contradictory ideas aimed at transforming the goals and ideals of American society and culture, and in particular of higher education. It introduced, on many American college campuses, the "Sovietization" of education, the subordination of standards of excellence and intellectual integrity to whatever happened to be the latest dogma of political correctness. Aside from anything else, the utopian aspirations of radical activists of the 1960s led to the smothering of academic freedom in American academic life. The effect that it had on public acceptance of Christianity and Christian moral values was devastating. Among other things, it led to the marginalization of Christian activity in many American colleges, the limitation of that activity to tiny "free speech zones," and the public ridiculing of Christian students by their professors.

Many people think sentimentally of the 1960s as a time of youthful idealism. They acknowledge that there was violence on American college campuses, often in protest against a war that was unpopular with students. But they tend to conflate such violence with the violence inflicted by southern white racists on African-American "freedom riders" who sought, by courageous activism, to desegregate the South. It is certainly true that African-American protesters and their white liberal student allies experienced violence, oppression, even murder at the hands of southerners who opposed racial integration and racial equality. But it is no less true that it was white radical and liberal activists who turned many American college campuses into locations of terror and destruction in the 1960s. I can personally recall a day when radical students and their hippie followers invaded the campus building where I had my office as a teaching assistant and for a brief period of time attempted to force a professor's fiftyish secretary to exit the building by climbing out of a rather high ground-floor window. I personally arrested, after a brief foot chase, one young radical who was attempting to set fire to the same building some months later.

The campus unrest of the sixties eventually died down. For one thing, American involvement in the war in Indochina eventually came to an end, as the antiwar protesters hoped. "Amerika"—the deliberate teutonic misspelling of America—had been publicly humbled in Asia, just as the radicals hoped it would be. For another, the radical students who had led the protests of the sixties needed to earn a living. Many of them went on to graduate school and then acquired jobs in the very universities that, at the height of the student unrest, they had tried to destroy. There they earned PhDs, obtained university jobs, and eventually acquired tenure, securing a position of comfort and power in the American academe. Robert Bork, President Reagan's nominee to the Supreme Court, who was scurrilously vilified by liberal opponents to his nomination (hence giving rise to a neologism, "to bork a person") has summed up what happened succinctly: "the sixties radicals are still with us, but now they do not paralyze the universities: they run the universities."[65]

Bork has shed light on a matter that has seemed something of a mystery to people who have tried to unravel what really happened in the sixties. He discerns the seed of campus unrest in an important document issued by the radical student group Students for a Democratic Society (SDS) in June of 1962. Meeting at a camp organized by the AFL-CIO in Port Huron, Michigan, SDS issued a ponderous and pedantic ideological tract of nearly twenty-six thousand words called the Port Huron Statement. For several years in the 1960s, SDS was active in organizing campus-based demonstrations against the Vietnam War. On many campuses there was violence or, where violence didn't actually occur, simply the threat of violence. One such standoff at Kent State University in Ohio culminated in the tragic shooting of four students by soldiers of the Ohio National Guard in May 1970. Americans were appalled by the shootings, and *Time* magazine headlined its cover-story on the shooting "Student Unrest." (My own story of arresting the youthful arsonist was briefly featured in it.) There was much national recrimination against the Ohio National Guard.

Though SDS was not directly blamed for the protests that provoked the shootings, the organization itself went through many splits in search of just the right formula to achieve its objectives most effectively. The most dramatic SDS development was the emergence of an SDS-originated group called the "Weathermen" or the Weather Underground. This conspiratorial cabal planned and executed violent actions against United States government property by bombing federal property. In one tragic development, three Weather Underground conspirators blew up themselves and the house they were using to manufacture bombs in Greenwich Village, New York, in March 1970.

Though a majority of Vietnam War student protesters did not engage in the organized violence against American institutions or individuals, a very large number of antiwar demonstrations were accompanied by violence against people or buildings. At Yale University on May 1, 1970, students rioted in the center of New Haven, broke windows, set fire to flyers they had brought to the demonstration, and damaged cars. The following day demonstrating students disrupted a campus dance, smashed windows of the ROTC building, and threw lighted railroad flares inside it. Over the same two days, turbulence and strikes took place on multiple American college campuses.

On dozens of other college campuses, the ROTC building, the administration building, or both were burned or bombed. For a brief period in 1970, the university in Seattle where I attended graduate school was rocked by bombings and disruptions. Seattle, in fact, was briefly thought of in 1970 as the "bombing capital of the United States."

As the Port Huron statement indicated, the underlying ideology of 1960s student radicalism was utopian. "Men have unrealized potential for self-cultivation, self-direction, self-understanding, and creativity," the Port Huron Statement read. "It is this potential that we regard as crucial and to which we appeal, not to the human potentiality for violence, unreason, and submission to authority."[66] According to some accounts, the original words of the statement, which was originally crafted by SDS leader Tom Hayden (later a member of California's state senate), had expressed the view that man was "infinitely perfectible," a view so radically secular that some of the delegates involved in the final draft objected on religious grounds, requiring Hayden to amend them to say "unrealized potential for self-cultivation."[67] In fact, belief in ultimate human malleability has always been a core component of totalitarianism. In George Orwell's novel *1984*, O'Brien, the torturer of protagonist Winston Smith, tells his victim, "You are imagining that there is something called human nature which will be outraged by what we do and will turn against us. But we create human nature. Men are infinitely malleable."[68] That, of course, was the frequently stated belief of tormentors of Chinese intellectuals during the Great Proletarian Cultural Revolution of 1966 to 1976.

Port Huron operated as a subtext for most of the student radical rebellion on American college campuses during the 1960s. The perfectibility of human nature was the creed of the leaders—sometimes stated, sometimes implicit. Its effect was to contaminate several generations of students who were later taught by the same radicals who had led the protests—now tenured faculty members—with the view that there were really no limits to human potential. Such a worldview, of course, amounted to a categorical rejection of the Christian view of humanity as powerfully stated in the seventeenth-century Calvinism of the Puritans: that humans are inherently flawed and desperately in need of divine assistance to prevent them from doing serious harm to themselves and other human beings.

Of course, the 1960s cannot be evaluated without referring to the "God is dead" movement in Christian theology. *Time* magazine featured a cover story in April 1966 entitled "Is God Dead?" The story was written by senior editor John Elson (a talented writer and editor under whom I later had the privilege of working) and elicited larger newsstand sales than any *Time* cover story in twenty years. The brouhaha over the cover itself (red letters against a black background) obscured a more important point: the emergence in the 1960s of a "death of God" theology that essentially denied not only the core of the Christian faith but any transcendental meaning to life itself. In effect, Christian theology, in some quarters, had rolled backward into full-blooded atheism like a wheelchair that has lost the person pushing it. This is how far liberal theology had come in its revolt against orthodoxy since America's earliest Puritan days.

Movements in theology, of course, were not the principle source of the erosion of Christianity in America. In many respects there were facets of the philosophical worldview in the 1960s that had nothing to do with political rebellion as such but came to influence American culture in a way that was deeply destructive of the Christian faith. The most important of these was the 1960s lifestyle adoption of the view that radical individualism—the emerging idol of a large sector of society—authorized unlimited sensual self-gratification. For a while, in the 1970s, there was an ugly social phenomenon called "wife-swapping": the deliberate practice of promiscuity by couples who under normal circumstances were friends with each other as married couples. More lasting, however, and more dangerous for people who wanted to live out the Christian faith, was the assumption by Hollywood and popular entertainment, from television soap operas to stand-up comedians, that it was now normative for men and women romantically drawn to each other to engage in sex outside marriage. Characters in television dramas who looked down on such behavior were routinely mocked or ridiculed, despite plain statistical evidence gathered by secular universities (i.e., not by Christian churches) that premarital cohabitation inevitably raised the likelihood of subsequent divorce.[69]

It is impossible to say to what extent these commonly accepted social trends eroded the core of commitment among America's Christians to live out the faith they had inherited from their forebears. They surely must have had some impact—how many ordinary Christians have been willing to resist social pressures exerted on them by their non-Christian friends? Probably not many. But it is now easier than it was two decades ago to see the huge damage inflicted upon American Christianity by the events and trends of the 1960s.

5

Countertrends

God Is Coming Back

Since the beginning of Christian history in the fourth decade of the first century AD, Christian communities have faced opposition and sometimes terrifying setbacks and persecutions. Christianity, whether you agree with it or not, has an exclusivist set of truth claims. Very few Christians would subscribe to the view that you can be "a little bit Christian" and a little bit of many other worldviews. Most Christians believe you are either a Christian or you are not, in the same way you are either pregnant or you are not. That doesn't mean that non-Christians cannot be influenced by Christians, as many have been, often to the benefit of the nearby Christian community. But in its growth and spread around the world, it has usually gone with the territory that not everyone wants to hear what Christians have always called the "Good News," the message that the almighty God, in an inexplicable act of love, generosity, and grace, became incarnated as a human being, was born and grew up as a human being, was put to death because people didn't like his story or actions, then was miraculously resurrected. His resurrection, Christians believe, is the ultimate authentication of the divinity of Jesus.

Jesus was a Jew, raised in a Jewish home and community, and all the first disciples were Jewish. But from both the Christian and later the Jewish point of view, the rejection by the Jewish religious establishment of Christian claims and testimonies resulted in the imprisonment and death of many early Christians (for example, see the persecution implemented by Paul in Acts 9:1–2). Periodic acts of violence against Christians took place in the first three centuries of Christian history. Yet the main resistance to the spread of Christianity in the Roman Empire initially came from the Romans themselves, with frequent and often brutal persecutions throughout the empire. The Roman government objected to Christianity for two reasons: it challenged the ethical validity of their pagan lifestyles, and Christians asserted that the imperial authority of the Roman Empire should be subordinated to what Christians called the lordship of Jesus Christ, a heavenly authority that trumped all earthly powers and authorities. This imperial opposition ended when Constantine conquered the Roman Empire in 311 and tolerated Christianity and other religions with the Edict of Toleration of 313. Constantine's favoring of Christianity, of course, led to the acquisition of political power by Christians. Many people consider that both the purity and the vigor of the Christian faith were seriously damaged by its exposure to the corruption of power.

Many people hold to a sort of fuzzy myth that after Christianity assumed the role of the established religion of the Roman Empire in the West and of what was to become the Byzantine empire in Constantinople, Europe was sort of Christianized overnight. That wasn't so at all. The last resistance of Nordic paganism in the northern Scandinavian regions was not overcome until the end of the twelfth century. The story of the heroic band of missionary evangelists who tamed barbarian Europe is brilliantly told in the classic by Christopher Dawson, *Religion and the Rise of Western Culture*.[1] Meanwhile, the Christians of the Mediterranean region had to face a new threat: the military, political, and cultural spread of Islam. By the end of the seventh century, long-established Christian communities had been all but wiped out after the Arab invasions.

This is not the place to review the history of Christianity's long historical conflict with Islam, nor of the ups and downs that Islam itself has undergone as the political and economic power of the (at least nominally) Christianized West in the past three centuries dominated Muslim parts of the world. Christian communities not only in the West but throughout the world have always faced opposition, sometimes a serious weakening, and occasionally almost total destruction. In the twentieth century, Christianity certainly experienced more direct persecution than in any previous age, with atheist-imbued Communist revolutions imposing brutal and despotic regimes on Russia, China, and other countries. In China today, Christianity is experiencing an ongoing campaign by the Communist regime to bring religious belief in general, and Christian belief in particular, under control. Numerous Chinese Christians have been martyred.

After observing, however, as we did in the previous chapter, the steady rise of opposition to Christianity in the United States from the mid-nineteenth century onward, it's important to grasp that even serious setbacks to Christianity can be, and have been, reversed, and to find, possibly, some hope and some strategy for dealing with the setbacks and opposing forces currently at work in America. The most dramatic example of a godless nation being utterly transformed by Christian evangelism is the story of England during the experience of the Wesleyan Revival (starting in the 1740s and lasting approximately a century).

Great Britain was a rising world power in the eighteenth century, but it was morally, socially, and politically corrupt. You could buy your way into parliament, and many did. A quarter of the entire British economy owed its existence to slavery and the slave trade. Crime, addiction to gin, and prostitution ravaged England's cities. England had the most notoriously brutal criminal code in Europe at the time. You could be hanged for stealing a few shillings. In fact, public executions were a prominent feature of popular entertainment in England at the time.

Then, like a spring-cleaning broom, the Wesleyan evangelical revival swept the country, permeating every class of society from aristocracy to the proletariat. In fact, it is broadly held by many historians that it was the Christian revival in the late eighteenth century that spared Great Britain from the horrors of a secular, atheist tyranny that came to France during the French Revolution. But the revival did not merely transform attitudes toward authority of ordinary workers: it led to the emergence of remarkable Christian reformers like William Wilberforce.

Wilberforce is correctly identified with the British parliament's abolition of the slave trade and then, days before Wilberforce himself died, of slavery itself within the British empire. Some people forget, however, that Wilberforce wrote down two goals in his journal in October of 1787: "God Almighty has set before me two great objects, the suppression of the Slave Trade and the Reformation of Manners."[2] Aside from the modest but important goal of abolishing slavery, Wilberforce did not want to instruct people on which knife and fork to use but to change their overall lifestyle from concern with pleasure and profit to concern with virtuous living.

Wilberforce's conversion came two decades or so after that of John Wesley, who had himself been converted (he had been before then a serious but nominal rather than "converted" Christian) after listening to a reading of Martin Luther's Preface to St. Paul's Letter to the Romans in a Moravian church in London in 1838. Wesley preached for years (with great opposition from both the established church and society secularists) to audiences in fields and barnyards throughout England and set in motion what became known as the Methodist revival, a huge evangelical transformation of English society. But the Moravian Christians in whose church Wesley was converted had been catapulted into successful evangelism not just in Moravia but also throughout the world by Christian activity in the town of Herrnhut, in the modern-day Czech Republic.

Wilberforce essentially succeeded; foreign visitors to England in the 1850s often complained how *boring* English social life was. You could not flirt with a British colleague's wife, let alone try to seduce his daughter. There remained much, of course, that was ugly in Victorian Britain. It took several decades to reform the worst outrages of the Industrial Revolution and to protect, for example, children from being tormented by work in factories and mines. Nor, of course, was sexual dalliance abolished. It remains a fact, however, that what is now called the Victorian age was largely a Christianized age. British imperialism and colonialism continued, but the watchful eyes of evangelical Christians in the British parliament were constantly campaigning for reforms to make British rule overseas more humane—in fact more Christian.

AMERICA'S SECULARIZATION AND ITS AFTERMATH

American college students at the end of the nineteenth century and beginning of the twentieth century who were interested in religion would be directed by liberal Christian, agnostic, or atheist faculty members toward courses that were virtually bereft of the doctrinal content of Christianity, or indeed of any religion. Along with agnostic and atheistic faculty colleagues, such liberal Christian professors almost certainly believed that religion would die a natural death as scientific knowledge and progress continued to develop. Many, perhaps most, academics believed that the world as a whole was moving inexorably towards secularism. Students who were interested in religious topics were encouraged to develop academic expertise in psychology, sociology, anthropology, or even folklore. There was a bare tolerance of religious faith at elite and large state universities. Most college students nevertheless failed to be drawn to the sort of "multicultural religion lite" that, as we saw in the previous chapter, was sometimes dangled as a potential topic for study before students who were interested in religion. Most American college students did not sink wholesale into a new swamp of unbelief, even though they may not have been especially pious or evangelically Christian in their worldviews. What did happen, however, was that the dominant faculty of many American elite universities developed in their intolerance toward Christianity in particular. They thus helped transform the American academy into one of the most intolerant locations of American intellectual life, multiple examples of which we have already seen.

Yet the fact is, the secularization project failed in American culture. Despite the hand-wringing of many top academics, Americans have remained stubbornly religious, as indeed most of the world has. It is always especially refreshing—because it is such a rare event—to witness a highly respected academic person acknowledge that the theory to which he contributed academic research for decades is, well, wrong. Such a man is Dr. Peter Berger, formerly at Boston University and currently Distinguished Professor of Church-State Studies at Baylor University in Texas.

In his introduction to a volume called *The Desecularization of the World*, Berger essentially reverses himself on the subject of the secularization of modern society. "My point," he wrote, "is that the assumption that we live in a secularized world is false. The world today, with some exceptions to which I will come presently, is as furiously religious as it ever was, and in some places more so than ever. This means that a whole body of literature by historians and social scientists loosely labeled secularization theory is essentially mistaken. In my earlier work I contributed to this literature. I was in good company. Most sociologists of religion had similar views, and we had good reasons for holding them. Some of the writings we produced still stand up."[3] Berger went on to say that he derived fun and amusement from seeing some of his pet theories upended by new scholarly findings.

Berger's good-natured self-ribbing is a testimony to both the honesty and the graciousness of the man. He hints heavily, though, at a disturbing phenomenon of the contemporary United States: a determined insistence among large academic institutions and philanthropic foundations (he mentions specifically the MacArthur Foundation with its heavily funded Fundamentalism Project) to treat strongly held religious convictions as though they were anthropologically exotic manifestations of a primitive culture. By contrast, Berger suggests, "strongly felt religion has always been around: what needs explanation is its absence rather than its presence." Impishly, he then adds, "Modern secularity is a much more puzzling phenomenon than all these religious explosions—if you will, the University of Chicago is a more interesting topic for sociology of religion than the Islamic schools of Qom."[4]

Berger makes another, more heavily weighted point. "By and large," he says, "religious communities have survived and even flourished to the degree that they have *not* tried to adapt themselves to the alleged requirements of a secularized world. To put it simply, experiments with secularized religion have generally failed: religious movements with beliefs and practices dripping with reactionary supernaturalism (the kind utterly beyond the pale at self-respecting faculty parties) have widely succeeded."[5]

Berger traces the secularization movement in the United States and Europe right back to the European Enlightenment. The idea, he said, was simple: "modernization necessarily leads to a decline of religion, both in society and in the minds of individuals. And it is precisely this key idea that has turned out to be wrong."[6] Other scholars of this phenomenon on American college campuses have a harsher view of the expulsion of religious ideas from the halls of the American academy. Hunter Baker, for example, interprets the secularization of America's campuses and big foundations not as happenstance consequences of mere changes in intellectual fashion but as the result of an intentional revolution. He cites Christian Smith, a sociologist of religion who argues that "public secularism achieved dominance by agency rather than by some natural movement of history." Baker concludes: "stated bluntly, the secularization of institutions in America was the result of an intentional revolution."

Baker, referring to Smith's findings, speaks of "an intentional program by secular activists. These activists 'were largely skeptical, freethinking, agnostic, atheist, or theologically liberal'; well-educated persons 'located mainly in knowledge production occupations' who 'generally espoused materialism, naturalism, positivism, and the privatization or extinction of religion.'"[7] For example, in 1905 Henry Smith Pritchett administered a Carnegie grant of $10,000,000 for professors' pensions. Pritchett was an ardent secularizer with a personal "faith in science." Pritchett deliberately excluded from the generous financial program any universities that had religious ties. The result: within four years of the Carnegie fund plan's coming into existence, twenty-eight colleges ended their relationships with sponsoring religious denominations. The board overseeing the fund consisted of major American university presidents (for example, Harvard's Charles Eliot, Columbia's Nicholas Murray Butler, Yale's Arthur T. Hadley, Stanford's David Starr Jordan, and Princeton's Woodrow Wilson). The board supervising the program approved the policy with the purpose of "standardizing American higher education" at least in part by secularizing it.

GOD MAY BE BACK

As I hope this account has made clear in the previous pages, the goal of driving religion, and more specifically Christianity, out of higher education altogether succeeded to a large extent.

Fortunately, it is not the end of the story. Observers other than Peter Berger and Hunter Baker have noted that the world in general not only shows no signs of succumbing to the secularization theory favored by many American academics but in fact is showing all kinds of signs of being as "furiously religious" as Berger maintained it had never stopped being.

The best-informed of all recent books documenting today's great resurgence of religion around the world is *God Is Back* by John Micklethwait and Adrian Wooldridge, editor-in-chief and Washington correspondent, respectively, of Britain's respected magazine *The Economist* (for some reason the magazine insists in calling itself a "newspaper"). The two seasoned journalists cover the waterfront of growing theistic religion on the world scene, from outreach-minded Muslims in the Persian Gulf to evangelical Christians in Korea and California.

Neither Micklethwait nor Wooldridge is an evangelical Christian. In fact, Wooldridge appears to be a good-natured agnostic and Micklethwait a half-hearted Roman Catholic. The more important point is that both are perceptive and energetic reporters who are bold enough to look for the big picture. What is striking about *God Is Back* is that though both reporters have spent a great deal of time in the United States and devote much space in the book to discussing the consequences of America's free enterprise-driven Christianity, the reporting doesn't start in America at all, but in China. *God Is Back* opens with a fascinating narrative of a group of Christians meeting for a private house-church gathering in Shanghai. The gathering is not illegal, because the Chinese government permits small groups of twenty-five or less to gather for prayer, meditation, or Bible reading, but groups do have to be careful not to attract too many participants or too much attention.[8]

The authors describe the Chinese attending: the host, a management consultant who used to work for Intel, two biotechnologists, a prominent academic, two ballet dancers, several successful entrepreneurs, and a chic young lady wearing a Che Guevara T-shirt. Though BMWs are parked outside and some of the participants have recently been on a Caribbean cruise, it's not in fact a gathering of Shanghai's super rich—just a cross-section of the myriad upscale Chinese professionals who find following Jesus an infinitely more satisfying way of living than an atheism-based hedonism.

The meeting described by Micklethwait and Wooldridge is a long one, with serious Bible study and earnest discussions of social issues punctuated by the singing of worship songs downloaded from a laptop on a coffee table. Part of the discussion, say the authors, veers off into a passionate attack on Darwinism, which, says host Wang (the management consultant who used to work at Intel), "is the biggest lie" because of its claims to be rigorous science. Yet the most striking part of the meeting comes towards the end, when Wang sums up the discussion and delivers his major point: Christianity is good for China because Christian nations have consistently been more powerful than non-Christian ones. "America grew strong because it was Christian," the authors paraphrase Wang. "The more Christian China becomes, the mightier it will be. If you want China to be a truly prosperous country, you must spread the Word to nonbelievers. If you are a patriotic Chinese, you have to be a Christian."[9]

Many outside observers of the Chinese scene have reported conversations with educated Chinese along these lines. At a lecture before a Washington, DC, audience in September of 2011, William Jeynes, professor of education at California State University at Long Beach, said that at a Harvard business conference several years ago, top Chinese CEOs insistently asked the Harvard professors questions about the relationship between Christianity and economics as it related to American business success. Apparently, the Harvard professors looked blank in relation to these questions. If any of them had read and paid attention to one of the most influential sociology and political science books of the last century and a half, Max Weber's *The Protestant Ethic and the Spirit of Capitalism*, there would have been no mystery in the Chinese inquiries. Weber, who is considered one of the most important voices in modern sociology, argued that the principle reason for economic success lay in the Calvinist understanding of work and life as a vocation, a divine calling that required highly disciplined, if not ascetic, personal behavior as emphasized in Protestantism shortly after the Reformation. In other words, according to Weber, the West had succeeded precisely where hard work and intelligence, combined with moral virtue, was encouraged in society.[10]

Chinese intellectuals had been saying similar things to the ideas reported by Professor Jeynes for some years. In 2001, a small tour group of Americans in Beijing were brought in to hear some comments by a prominent member of the Chinese Academy of Social Sciences, one of China's major government-backed intellectual think tanks. The tourists were tired and weren't really expecting much from the meeting with the scholar because it had been arranged at short notice, but what he said astonished them. "One of the things we were asked to look into," he said (presumably referring to the academy's bosses),

> was what accounted for the success, in fact, the pre-eminence of the West all over the world. We studied everything we could from the historical, political, economic, and cultural

> perspective. At first, we thought it was because you had more powerful guns than we had. Then we thought it was because you had the best political system. Next we focused on your economic system. But in the past twenty years, we have realized that the heart of your culture is your religion: Christianity. That is why the West has been so powerful. The Christian moral foundation of social and cultural life was what made possible the emergence of capitalism and then the successful transition to democratic politics. We don't have any doubt about this.[11]

This comment by a Chinese social scientist has been quoted many times in books about China and about global Christianity. The reason is simple: the Chinese are first and foremost a pragmatic people. Though they are still under the political control of a Communist Party that claims to subscribe to the economic theories of a nineteenth-century German, their best brains recognize reality when they see it. This may explain why Christianity is tolerated and sometimes even encouraged in China at the grass roots but is savagely repressed when any particular church organization appears to have grown too big or too independent. China recognizes the value of a religious faith that teaches moral self-restraint even as their capitalism-fueled economic success has given rise to worrying examples of economic and political corruption and other manifestations of moral decadence. Professor Jeynes said that Chinese personal morality is so out of control that a Chinese leader expressed worry to him that if it were not reversed, China's economic expansion might be at risk.[12] The reason for China's persistent repression of individual Christian leaders is the fear that if they became too prominent, they might form the vanguard of a movement that eventually would discard Communism itself.

PHILOSOPHY REDISCOVERS GOD

While none of this information, interesting though it is, appears likely to harbinger a new flowering of the Christian faith in the United States, there are some interesting signs of new sprouts of faith in the ground. Most interesting of all may be the countertrend to the blanket secularism that has occurred in the academic community. In one of the most surprising trends of all, American university philosophy departments are now heavily populated by professors who believe in God and who may quite likely be Christians. "By the second half of the twentieth century," the author Quentin Smith argues, "universities and colleges had become in the main secularized. The standard (if not exceptionless) position in each field, from physics to psychology, assumed or involved arguments for a naturalist world-view; departments of theology or religion aimed to understand the meaning and origins of religious writings, not to develop arguments against naturalism." The situation drastically changed, however, according to Smith, after an influential book by the Christian philosopher Alvin Plantinga (*God and Other Minds*) published in 1966. Smith says that "the secularization of mainstream academia began to unravel upon the publication of Plantinga's influential book on realist theism."

The result: an apparent mini-revolution in American universities' philosophy departments. Writing in 2001, Smith said that "perhaps one-quarter or one-third of philosophy departments are theists, with most being orthodox Christians. . . . God is not 'dead' in academia; he returned to life in the late 1960s and is now alive and well in his last academic stronghold, philosophy departments."[13]

The resurgence of theism as a credible intellectual worldview on American college campuses is something that will have to be fought for department by department and, in places where the hostility toward Christianity is particularly virulent, professor by professor. Yet one of the most interesting developments that is very positive for the future of Christianity in America is the growth of student evangelical ministries and student Christian groups across the country. Perhaps the best known of these groups is Campus Crusade for Christ (which has recently changed its name to Cru), an organization founded by evangelist Bill Bright in 1951. Campus Crusade claims 25,000 staff members worldwide and 3,300 staffers on 1,140 campuses in the United States alone. Campus Crusade is probably most famous for its 1979 movie production popularly known as *The Jesus Film*, which has 1,090 translations and probably has been seen now by more people in the world than any other movie ever, perhaps by more than two billion.

The longest-established American campus evangelical organization is InterVarsity Christian Fellowship, founded in the United States in 1941 after migrating to Canada from its original base, England, where it was founded in 1877. InterVarsity is smaller than Cru but carefully keeps track of numbers of students showing interest in its activities. This is important for several reasons. According to the *Almanac of Higher Education*, the number of Americans enrolling as students in American colleges and universities has been on an upward trend for years. The annual reports that undergraduate enrollment increased by 38 percent from 1999 to 2009. The total number of United States college students passed twenty million for the first time in history in 2009.

According to InterVarsity, the Higher Education Institute reports, intriguingly, that 75 percent of college freshmen are "searching for meaning and purpose in life" as they begin their college career. InterVarsity says that its mission on campus "is to help students complete their search for meaning and purpose in life through a personal relationship with the Lord Jesus Christ." The number of students finding new faith in Jesus Christ through the witness of InterVarsity staff and students, the organization says, has increased by 30 percent over the past five years.[14]

The internet is full of websites dedicated to transforming campuses in the United States and around the world through concentrated prayer. For example, the Luke 18 Project creates videos that describe the effort exerted by the group as "a nameless, faceless, grassroots movement of prayer and fasting" to turn the world around. "The Luke 18 Project," says Brian Kim on-camera, "seeks to answer the question of what will happen when an entire generation begins to pray and ask for breakthrough in their nation in an entire generation."[15] Another group, 24-7 Prayer, claims to have maintained a twenty-four hour a day prayer and fasting program around the world since it was initiated by a single prayer group in Chichester, England, in 1999. The movement says it has spread to more than one hundred nations around the world.[16]

Jaeson Ma says he has planted between four hundred and five hundred "houses of prayer" on college campuses across the United States, as well as his own group of 24-7 prayer groups on campus. Ma is an Asian-American who at one time was a student at San Jose State University in a class with some 250 other students. According to him, the instructor in a mocking way asked anyone who believed that Jesus Christ was the Son of God to raise his hand. Ma said he was the only one in the entire lecture hall who had the courage to do so. Jaeson Ma's book describing his own spiritual experience and his vision is called *The Blueprint*. One of the campus activities Ma began to establish in the 2000 decade was 24-7 campus prayer ministries. In the book, he cites a passage from his personal blog entry from February 10, 2006: "It *broke out* last night from 11:00 p.m. to 3 a.m. at UCLA. Students started showing up and a spirit of revival fell out of nowhere. Students all over the room started *crying out* to God for the UCLA campus, and their prayers kept going on for a few hours. There were student leaders from different campus fellowship in the room. It was powerful. I thought I was on Prayer Mountain in Korea or at an underground Chinese house church prayer meeting."[17]

Ma is only 31, yet he has accomplished much in working with other Christian leaders not only to direct young Christians into missionary efforts overseas but also in attempting to galvanize young American Christians to make a major impact on evangelism and to utilize social media and the internet and the contemporary youth culture to reach young people where they are. Ma, whose blog (www.jaesonma.blogspot.com) sometimes receives thousands of hits daily, is very conscious of the need to use every possible form of social media to impact America's young people for Christ. He says,

> You have got to reach them where they are at. It's always been where they are at for me. Where are they? Most of them are hooked up to their iPods, watching YouTube, etc. They are not in a church building. More than 85 percent of young people don't go back to church after they leave high school. Everything is up there for the taking. I've got to reach them on Facebook. The method of reaching people for the Gospel has changed. The method my father did in the 1970s is not going to work. The Gospel never changes but the method of communicating it changes.[18]

Ma lives and spends a great deal of time organizing and preaching on the West Coast, yet in many ways the most intriguing development in the effort to turn America's colleges back to the Christian faith is a very recent movement right in the heart of the Ivy League in New England. Christian Union, founded in 2002, operates on the premise that of the twenty-one million students currently enrolled on American college campuses, a tiny segment of no more than one hundred thousand students on eight Ivy League Campuses (Harvard, Yale, Princeton, Cornell, Penn, Dartmouth, Columbia, Brown) will produce 50 percent of the top leaders of corporate America. In fact, 50 percent of the CEOs of America's top ten internet companies are graduates from these Ivy League schools.

In spite of the disproportionate influence of graduates from Ivy League universities in top leadership positions in the corporate world, academic life, and government, the Christian Union uncovered statistics showing that 93 percent of the students on those eight select Ivy League campuses have no regular Christian faith input in their lives whatsoever. The website of Christian Union says that "the proportion of Christian involvement and impact on these campuses has not changed in 50 years. There is no good reason to expect that America will substantively change spiritually in the next 50 years if these campuses are not dramatically changed in our present day." The site adds, "Currently, these campuses are extremely secular in their outlook, representing a slow-motion train wreck that has been negatively impacting our country and world for a generation."[19]

Christian Union has already organized several conferences open to Ivy League students. At a conference in April 2011, held at a hotel in Cambridge and described as "one of the largest gathering of Ivy League Christians in history," Christian sociologist and scholar Os Guinness posed these questions to his audience: "Can we really change the world? Is it just a pious phrase, or do you seriously expect there can be real change? Are you committed to winning back the West again for our Lord?"[20] Christian Union hopes to provide an affirmative answer by nurturing an entire generation of Ivy League students through well-organized and well-attended Bible study programs on campus and through high-octane mentoring by staffers with a high educational level and often extensive life experience.

If returning the Ivy League college campuses to their origins centered in a Christian worldview is important, so is the enormous challenge of drawing the attention of Americans away from a hedonistic and sometimes selfish lifestyle back to health-giving spiritual goals. There are too many different kinds of ministries operating out of America's galaxy of churches to describe in detail how the re-evangelization of America is being envisaged in all its varieties, but there are some telling vignettes of vigorous, church-based activity in process.

One of the most interesting developments in American evangelism is the rediscovery of Calvinism, the theological worldview that powered, after all, the thinking of New England's earliest Christian communities and that exerted a major influence on the founders even after Calvinism proper ceased to be the theology of choice for many American Christians. A leading voice in this movement is John Piper, pastor for preaching at Bethlehem Baptist Church in Minneapolis. Piper is famous for his concept of "Christian hedonism," which he articulates in this way: "God is most glorified in us when we are most satisfied in him." Piper in 1986 wrote a book called *Desiring God: Meditations of a Christian Hedonist*[21] and founded Desiring God Ministries. The purpose of this, Piper says, is "to spread a passion for the supremacy of God in all things for the joy of all peoples through Jesus Christ."[22]

Piper's Christian message is indeed hedonistic, though not in the worldly sense of the term. "We stress a joyful, big view of God," Piper says. "He's great, he's majestic, he's holy, he's absolute. You don't mess with him. He's the creator of the universe. Yet, as powerful as he is, he desires that we should take delight in him." While speaking at large Christian conferences, he has elicited a surprisingly enthusiastic response among young people. He says he's "stunned" that there is "such a significant awakening among young people."

Piper's version of the gospel might offend some people. For one thing, he is unsympathetic to radical feminists or even the generalized post-1960s view that men and women are entirely the same. His view of male-female relations is what is sometimes called "complementarian," the view that men and women are actually different from each other—"I was called obscene in the seventies for saying such things," he chuckles—and that the Bible teaches that men should be in leadership roles in church settings. Piper says he sees signs of spiritual resurgence among the Southern Baptists. "I'm calling men to be spiritual warriors and to lay down their lives," he says. "I've only known one kind of truth."[23] He must be doing something right. When Piper became a pastor at his Minneapolis church in 1980, it had just three hundred members. Now it has about three thousand.

Another Calvinist with a difference is Mark Driscoll, founding pastor of Mars Hill Church in Seattle, long regarded as one of the least churchgoing cities in the United States and, in the eyes of many observers, the body-piercing capital of the United States. Driscoll was born again at nineteen and says God audibly spoke to him. "He told me to marry Grace [a pretty young woman he had met in high school], preach the Bible, to plant churches and train men." He married Grace (with whom he now has five children) and, at twenty-five, founded Mars Hill. Since that time the church has grown from a handful of people in the 1970s to a multi-venue establishment that draws as many as 7,500 people on a given Sunday.

Driscoll is, like Piper, a Calvinist, emphasizing that human beings are totally depraved in their natural state, but nevertheless, some are predestined by God to salvation. Yet Driscoll differs from Piper in challenging head-on the cultural trendsetting that characterizes many people who live in and around Seattle. Unlike many Protestant evangelicals, he does not require new converts to abandon smoking and drinking, much less to give up tattoos. In fact, some members of his regular congregation are tattoo artists. Driscoll's congregation in the past has included—and probably still does—characters who were once strippers and prostitutes. In an amusing account in a video on his website (www.marshill.com) of how he dealt with new converts in the early days of his ministry, Driscoll recalls confronting a new Christian who balked at destroying or giving away his vintage pornography collection. "But it includes Nazi porn," the new Christian protested. Driscoll insisted it had to go anyway.

Driscoll disdains feminists and indeed emphasizes "complementarian" relationships between men and women: both genders, he says, are spiritually equal, but God has designated different roles for men and women. He is also strongly opposed to the traditional evangelical projections of a Jesus who is "meek and mild," something of a milquetoast, and not the sort of radical masculine dude he believes Christian men should aspire to become. A *New York Times* story on Mars Hill Church in 2009 described Driscoll as "evangelicalism's bête noire." Perhaps he is, but it's worth asking how many other preachers are having the same dramatic impact on young people who have embraced the spiked hair and arm-tattoo lifestyle.[24]

An insightful observer of what is going on among the Southern Baptists mentioned by Piper is Richard Land, president of the Ethics and Religious Liberty Commission of the Southern Baptist Convention. Though he is careful in public statements to avoid political partisanship, Land was present in July 2011 when Texas governor Rick Perry convened a day of prayer and fasting for the United States. The call to national prayer was criticized on several fronts, but Land says that more than half of the estimated crowd of thirty-five thousand people were twenty-five years old and younger. "I see tremendous energy in the young people," he comments. "I see no limit to the growth of the charismatic movement [sometimes referred to as the neo-Pentecostal movement]. I see growth in terms of seminary enrollment. Today's seminarians are like green berets, spiritual navy seals. They are more dedicated, more zealous, less intimidated by the culture. When I was in seminary, I was pretty traditional."[25]

One location where this newfound zeal has borne fruit is, oddly enough, Manhattan. Growth in the number of evangelical Manhattanites has not been spectacular—from 1 percent in 1990 to 3 percent today—but the growth in the number of evangelical churches at the heart of New York City has been explosive. Some 40 percent of all Manhattan's evangelical churches were established since 2000, and at one point in 2009, an evangelical church was being established every Sunday. One obvious explanation is the changing demography of the city with endless waves of new immigrants, many of them being evangelical and Pentecostal Hispanics. It's important to note, however, that one evangelical church, Redeemer Presbyterian, has established in a space of a few years no fewer than 75 startup Redeemer communities throughout town. Redeemer is led by a prolific writer and broadly known Christian speaker named Timothy Keller. Keller has helped start more than 175 new churches of various denominational backgrounds in New York City since he first pioneered Redeemer in 1989.

Other cities in America have experienced almost exponential church growth in recent years. In Dallas, famed African-American church leader Bishop T. D. Jakes is senior pastor at The Potter's House, a church with a membership of thirty thousand people and average Sunday worship service attendance of eight thousand to twelve thousand. Jakes says that he and other church leaders were so surprised by the number of people who tuned in to worship services via the internet that he had to increase staffing just to manage this part of his church outreach. He thinks the talk of a downturn in churchgoing and church membership mentioned in the 2009 *Newsweek* article "The End of Christian America" (see chap. 1) is not matched by what he has noticed in the attendance and membership at his own church. He says he is pleasantly surprised by the greater degree of media interest in what his and other churches are doing in the community. He is, nevertheless, convinced that the Christian community in the United States is up against a reporting bias that is significantly prejudiced against Christian belief. "The media tends to be liberal," he says. "It is so difficult for people who embrace liberal ideas not to demonize people who embrace moderate or even conservative views (on spiritual issues)."[26]

Franklin Graham, son of famous evangelist Billy Graham, is a lot more dour about the spiritual antagonism in America toward the gospel—not just from the media but also from the government itself. The younger Graham has been disinvited from scheduled prayer functions at the Pentagon because of opposition from Islamic chaplains within the Chaplain Corps (Graham has made some comments extremely critical of Islam). Graham believes that when he faces opposition either from government officials or from the media about his preaching, he is encountering a literally devilish opposition. He explains, "I believe the Bible, and when I read the Scripture, I read about the spirit of the Antichrist. The Antichrist spirit is in the world today. Secularism is nothing more than the Antichrist. You can do anything you want, but don't mention Jesus. It's now permeated our government. It's in our media, in our entertainment." Graham appears to subscribe to dispensationalist theology, which holds that America and the world are on a downhill course that will be reversed only when Christ returns at the second coming. Before that time, according to dispensationalists, there will be a one-world government and a one-world monetary system. Franklin Graham says he's not discouraged by these possible future trends in the United States and the world because, as he says, "the Bible is true" and Christians are therefore destined in the end to be on the winning team.[27]

But if you are a Christian who is not a dispensationalist, not to mention if you are just a regular person who is not (yet) a Christian, however attractive the message of God's love and Jesus's offer of forgiveness of sin may be, the prospect of increasing gloom until the light of the second coming suddenly flashes into the world might not tempt you immediately to identify with the Christian team. It is thus worth recalling that many English people shared a rather similar despairing view of life in England in, say, 1750, before the Methodist revival, as we observed earlier, began to reinject Christian virtue into the country. It is interesting to ask whether slavery would ever have been abolished in

Great Britain if Wilberforce had been a dispensationalist. (In fact, the doctrine did not really become widespread in either England or the United States until the late nineteenth century.)

Wilberforce had been converted to active Christian belief by a follower of John Wesley. Wesley himself had been converted during a sermon in a London church organized by Moravian Christians. Who were these Moravians?

They were Protestants who had been cruelly persecuted by Roman Catholic authorities and had taken refuge on the estate of a Protestant Czech nobleman, Nikolaus Ludwig von Zinzendorf. The Moravian refugees, later called Herrnhutters after the name of the town near the estate, began a 24-7 prayer meeting that lasted a century and stirred up Protestant Christian missionary activity throughout the world. Thus when Loren Cunningham, founder of the world's largest youth mission organization, Youth with a Mission, visited the Zinzendorf estate a few years ago, he was eager to emphasize the connection between enthusiastic young evangelicals from all over the world and the upsurge of prayer among the Moravians. "Three years ago," he told me, "bands of YWAM-ers felt they should return to Herrnhut and rediscover the emphasis on prayer. We are seeing the classic example of history when movements of God are taking place among young people. I see signs of a new awakening. We are on the brink of an exponential growth in coming to Jesus."[28]

How might such a movement start? Chances are that there might first be scattered mini-revivals in already-existing churches. Often the first signs of a major change are really quite small. At a typical daily chapel service in mid-September at Patrick Henry College, for example, the speaker was a senior named Brett Harris who, with his twin brother Alex Harris, has already written a book and founded a website (TheRebelution.com, "a teenage rebellion against low expectations"). Harris was challenging chapel-going students (Patrick Henry is a private Christian college and chapel attendance is mandatory) to move beyond mere formalism in their Christian behavior. He asked all the students to write on anonymous note cards their answers to these three questions:

1. How often do you pray when no one has asked you to or is expecting you to?
2. How often do you read the Bible just because you want to?
3. How often do you obey God without being urged to do so by someone else?

Harris, who had gotten permission in advance from the college authorities to take this action, then asked students who had written "yes" to the question at the end, "Are you born again?" to stand up before all their peers.

Technically, every student attending the college could have answered yes because the college requires prospective students to make a statement of Christian faith before being admitted, but Harris suspected that many students had merely gone through the motions (albeit sincerely) without ever experiencing the change of heart that Christians are supposed to experience when they become believers. To his amazement, twenty students, from freshmen to seniors, rose sheepishly to their feet.

Senior Jeremy Siblerud from Kalispell, Montana, was one of them. "I actually started shaking," he recalls. "I really heard the voice of the Holy Spirit. I'd never felt anything like that before. Ever since, I have a sense that Christ is in me." Siblerud says that he and his family attended an evangelical church in Montana, but though he had gone through all the required motions of

Christian commitment, he had "felt like a Pharisee." He adds, "Most of America seems to have been immunized to the Christian faith. People kind of understand it, but they don't get the heart of it."[29] Jeremy's shaking may eventually fade from his memory, but something seemed to have happened in that chapel service. Perhaps it needs to happen all over America.

It may be worth recalling what a Chinese economist, Zhao Xiao, yet another of China's observers of the American Christian connection, said. The churches, he remarked, "and only churches, are the very core that binds America together."[30] In an interview with PBS *Frontline* reporter Evan Osnos, he added, "We know that America is a country founded by Puritans. And Puritans, their dream of coming to America was the need to establish a city on a hill, to let the entire world see the glory of Jesus Christ, whom they believed in. So their purpose for doing business was for the glory of God. If my motivation for doing business is the glory of God, there is a motivation that transcends profits."[31]

Yet Zhao Xiao also served a sober warning to China, quoting an angry poem:

> *Be in awe of the invincible might,*
> *Be in awe of the lightning,*
> *And be in awe of the thunder in the sky.*

Without this awe, Zhao said, China could not succeed or be an effective Christian nation. "Only through awe can we be saved."[32]

John Winthrop would have shared the same thought. And if it is true for China, it must surely be true for America.

Acknowledgments

I owe an incalculable debt to Chad Allen, editorial director of Baker Books, for coming up with the idea for this book and for nurturing it along. He was especially patient after delays, largely induced by physical ailments, forced the postponement of delivery of the manuscript. I'd like to thank Rebecca Cooper for her careful and thoughtful perusal of the manuscript.

It is difficult to remember all the individuals who have contributed to some ideas in this book—though certainly not to any of its flaws—but I should start with Dr. Graham Walker, president of Patrick Henry College, where I teach. His insights into the formation of American Christian ideas were always insightful. Other Patrick Henry colleagues, especially Robert Spinney and Laura McCollum, generously lent me books for long periods, perhaps doubtful about whether they would ever get them back. I also thank Dr. Thomas S. Kidd, associate professor of history at Baylor University.

My good friend Os Guinness was broad and deep with his insights. Os is justifiably respected for his ability to grasp the large historical picture.

Many of the people actually mentioned and sometimes quoted in the book were thoughtful in responding to my requests for their own views on the topic: Loren Cunningham, Franklin Graham, Chuck Colson, T. D. Jakes, Richard Land, Al Mohler, John Piper, and many others.

Jeannie Light, a deacon at Truro Episcopal Church in Fairfax, Virginia, provided great encouragement and moral and spiritual support.

Last, I need to express gratitude to my wife Charlene, not only for putting up with the inevitable reclusiveness that writing a book induces but also for very helpful and important contributions to the editorial content. As a number of friends have commented, she is one of the best editors in the world.

Notes

Chapter 1 Not a Christian Nation?

1. Barack Hussein Obama, White House press office, Joint Press Availability with President Gul of Turkey, April 6, 2009, http://www.whitehouse.gov/the_press_office/Joint-Press-Availability-With-President-Obama-And-President-Gul-Of-Turkey/.

2. "Obama Declares We Are Not a Christian Nation," The Lonely Conservative, April 7, 2009, http://lonelyconservative.com/2009/04/obama-declares-we-are-not-a-christian-nation/.

3. Debbie Schlussel, "Obama to Muslim Turkey: America is NOT a 'Christian Nation'; Forgets Turkish History and Current Developments; But Statements No More Pandering Than Bush's," DebbieSchlussel.com, April 6, 2009, http://www.debbieschlussel.com/5025/obama-to-muslim-turkey-america-is-not-a-christian-nation-forgets-turkish-history-and-current-developments-but-statements-no-more-pandering-than-bushs/.

4. David Brody, "Obama to CBN News: We're No Longer Just a Christian Nation," CBN.com, July 30, 2007, http://cbn.com/CBNnews/204016.aspx.

5. John Eidsmoe, "Obama: America Not a Christian Nation," *The New American*, April 15, 2009, http://www.thenewamerican.com/usnews/election/1003.

6. All critics cited here are quoted at "Fox News Figures Outraged over Obama's 'Christian nation' comment," Media Matters for America, April 9, 2009, http://mediamatters.org/research/200904090033.

7. Warner Todd Huston, "What Are We If NOT a Christian Nation?" RedState.com, April 8, 2009, http://www.redstate.com/warner_todd_huston/2009/04/08/what-are-we-if-not-a-christian-nation/.

8. Michael Lind, "America Is Not a Christian Nation," Salon, April 14, 2009, http://www.salon.com/news/opinion/feature/2009/04/14/christian_nation.

9. Randall Balmer, "America Is Not a Christian Nation and Evangelicals Are Not Hard Right," *Huffington Post*, January 12, 2010, http://www.huffingtonpost.com/randall-balmer/america-is-not-a-christia_b_420287.html.

10. Jim Wallis, *God's Politics: Why the Right Gets It Wrong and the Left Doesn't Get It* (San Francisco: HarperSan Francisco, 2006).

11. Cited in Jon Meacham, "The End of Christian America," *Newsweek*, April 13, 2009, http://www.thedailybeast.com/newsweek/2009/04/03/the-end-of-christian-america.html.

12. Ibid.

13. Ibid.

14. Barry A. Kosmin and Ariela Keysar, "American Religious Identification Survey (ARIS 2008): Summary Report" (Hartford, CT: March 2009), http://commons.trincoll.edu/aris/files/2011/08/ARIS_Report_2008.pdf, 6.

15. Meacham, "End of Christian America."

16. Ibid.

17. Cal Thomas and Ed Dobson, *Blinded by Might: Can the Religious Right Save America?* (Grand Rapids: Zondervan, 1999).

18. T. David Gordon, "The Decline of Christianity in the West? A Contrarian View," *Ordained Servant Online*, May 2007, http://www.opc.org/os.html?article_id=44. Quoted at http://oldlife.org/2009/04/30/the-end-of-christian-america/.

19. Darryl Hart on http://oldlife.org/2009/04/30/the-end-of-christian-america/

20. E. J. Dionne Jr., "A Resilient Christianity," *Washington Post*, April 12, 2009, http://www.washingtonpost.com/wp-dyn/content/article/2009/04/10/AR2009041002604.html.

21. John Fea, "The End of Christian America?" *The Way of Improvement Leads Home* (blog), April 12, 2009, http://www.philipvickersfithian.com/2009/04/end-of-christian-america.html.

22. Douglas V. Gibbs, "Newsweek's Headline, 'The End of Christian America,' echoes Obama's 'We are not a Christian Nation,'" *Canada Free Press*, April 9, 2009, http://www.canadafreepress.com/index.php/article/10086.

23. Todd Strandberg, "The End of Christian America? Not Really," *Bible Prophecy Blog*, April 20, 2009, http://www.bibleprophecyblog.com/2009/04/end-of-christian-america-not-really.html.

24. Hank Hanegraaff, telephone interview with the author, Spring 2011.

25. The authors, and their books, in alphabetical order, were Richard Dawkins, *The God Delusion* (London: Bantam, 2006); Daniel Dennett, *Breaking the Spell* (New York: Penguin Books, 2007); Sam Harris, *Letter to a Christian Nation* (New York: Vintage Books, 2006); and Christopher Hitchens, *God Is Not Great: How Religion Poisons Everything* (New York: Twelve, 2007).

26. His complete works are available online at the Robert Green Ingersoll website, http://www.robertgreeningersoll.org/.

27. Alliance Defense Fund, "Religious Freedom," http://www.alliancedefensefund.org/ReligiousFreedom.

28. "About the ACLU," American Civil Liberties Union, http://www.aclu.org/about-aclu-0.

29. "Religion and Belief," American Civil Liberties Union, http://aclu.org/religion-belief.

30. Matt Staver, interview with the author, October 5, 2010.

31. "Colorado School District Urges Churchgoing," *Freethought Today* 24, no. 8 (October 2007), available online at http://www.ffrf.org/publications/freethought-today/articles/Colorado-School-District-Urges-Churchgoing/.

32. Cited in Annie Youderian, "Pledge OK in NH Public Schools, 1st Circuit Rules," Courthouse News Service, November 15, 2010, http://www.courthouse news.com/2010/11/15/31863.htm.

33. Alliance Defense Fund, "Defending Religious Freedom," http://www.alliance defensefund.org/ReligiousFreedom.

34. Alliance Defense Fund, http://oldsite.alliancedefensefund.org/issues/reli giousfreedom/Default.aspx.

35. Jay Sekulow, interview with the author, October 21, 2010.

36. Michael Medved, *Hollywood vs. America: The Explosive Bestseller That Shows How—and Why—the Entertainment Industry Has Broken Faith with Its Audience* (New York: Harper Paperbacks, 1993).

37. Cited in Brad O'Leary, *America's War on Christianity* (New York: WND Books, 2010), 88.

38. Jim Garlow, interview with the author, September 30, 2010.

39. Jay Sekulow, interview with the author, October 21, 2010.

40. David Limbaugh, *Persecution: How Liberals Are Waging a War Against Christianity* (New York: Perennial Books, 2004) and Brad O'Leary, *America's War on Christianity* (New York: WND Books, 2012).

41. Cited in Limbaugh, *Persecution*, 5.

42. Cited in ibid., 276.

43. Cited in ibid., 54.

Chapter 2 Where Are the Christians in America?

1. Andrew Kohut et al., *Millennials: A Portrait of Generation Next* (Washington, DC: Pew Research Center, 2010). Hereafter referred to as the Pew Forum report.

2. Ibid., 3.

3. Ibid.

4. Ibid., 51.

5. Polls by Rasmussen, Pew, and Gallup all provided evidence that younger Americans, in 2009 and 2010, were leaning toward more favorable attitudes toward socialism. Pew found that the percentage of young Americans finding socialism positive, 43 percent, was identical to the percentage who found capitalism positive. See Charles Derber, "Pew Poll: Support for Socialism Growing in US," The Kasama Project, May 24, 2010, http://kasamaproject.org/2010/05/24/20014/.

6. Pew Forum report, 3.

7. Ibid., 101.

8. Ibid., 87.

9. Ibid., 97.

10. Ibid., 14–15.

11. Ibid., 106.

12. Robert Wuthnow, *After the Baby Boomers* (Princeton, NJ: Princeton University Press, 2005), 17.

13. Naomi Schaefer Riley, *God in the Quad* (New York: St. Martin's Press, 2005), 3.

14. Christian Smith with Melinda Lundquist Denton, *Soul-Searching: The Religious and Spiritual Lives of American Teenagers* (New York: Oxford University Press, 2005).

15. Christian Smith with Patricia Snell, *Souls in Transition: The Religious and Spiritual Lives of Emerging Adults* (New York: Oxford University Press, 2009).

16. Ibid., 154.

17. Ibid., 145.

18. Pew Forum report, 41.

19. Wuthnow, *After the Baby Boomers*, 15.

20. Barna Group, "Most Twentysomethings Put Christianity on the Shelf Following Spiritually Active Teen Years," September 11, 2006, http://www.barna.org/barna-update/article/16-teensnext-gen/147-most-twentysomethings-put-christianity-on-the-shelf-following-spiritually-active-teen-years.

21. Ibid.

22. Ibid.

23. Ibid.

24. David Kinnaman and Gabe Lyons, *UnChristian: What a New Generation Really Thinks about Christianity . . . and Why It Matters* (Grand Rapids: Baker, 2007).

25. Ibid., 11.

26. Ibid., 24.

27. Ibid., 26.

28. Ibid., 27.

29. Smith and Snell, *Souls in Transition*, 188.

30. Ibid., 155.

31. Ibid., 293.

32. Ibid.

33. Ibid., 101.

34. Ibid., 288.

35. Ibid., 293.

36. Ibid.

37. Kenda Creasy Dean, *Almost Christian: What the Faith of Our Teenagers Is Telling the American Church* (New York: Oxford University Press, 2010).

38. Ibid., Kindle edition, location 130.

39. Ibid.

40. Ibid., location 117.

41. Ibid., location 98–104.

42. Cited in Smith and Snell, *Souls in Transition*, 288.

43. Ibid.

44. Lillian Kwon, "Falwell: Measurements of Success in Ministry are Messed Up," *The Christian Post*, May 18, 2010, http://www.christianpost.com/news/falwell-measurements-of-success-in-ministry-are-messed-up-45219/.

45. H. Richard Niebuhr, *The Kingdom of God in America* (New York: Harper, 1937), 193; cited in Smith and Snell, *Souls in Transition*, 288.

Chapter 3 Was America Ever a Christian Nation?

1. Peter Marshall and David Manuel, *The Light and the Glory* (Grand Rapids: Revell, 2009).

2. Ibid., 19.

3. George Washington, "First Inaugural Address in the City of New York," in *Inaugural Addresses of the Presidents of the United States* (New York: Bartleby.com, 2001–2009), http://www.bartleby.com/124/pres13.html.

4. John Quincy Adams, letter of April 27, 1837, *The Historical Magazine and Notes and Queries Concerning the Antiquities, History and Biography of America*, Vol. IV (New York: Charles B. Richardson and Co., 1860).

5. Richard Dawkins, *River Out of Eden: A Darwinian View of Life*, The Science Masters Series (New York: BasicBooks, 1996), 133.

6. Mark A. Noll, Nathan O. Hatch, and George M. Marsden, *The Search for Christian America* (Colorado Springs: Helmers & Howard, 1989), 17.

7. John Fea, *Was America Founded as a Christian Nation?* (Louisville: Westminster John Knox, 2011).

8. Ibid., 174.

9. Ibid., 82.

10. Cited in R. B. Nye and J. E. Morpurgo, *A History of the United States, Volume One: The Birth of the USA* (Harmondsworth, Middlesex, England: Penguin Books, 1955), 24.

11. Cited in Charles Dudley Warner, ed., *Captain John Smith*, Easyread edition (Sydney, Australia: ReadHowYouWant, 2007).

12. "First Hand Accounts of Virginia, 1575–1705," Virtual Jamestown, http://etext.lib.virginia.edu/etcbin/jamestown-browse?id+J1047.

13. Cited in Nye and Morpurgo, *History of the United States*, 28.

14. "Mayflower Compact (1620)," MayflowerHistory.com, http://www.mayflowerhistory.com/PrimarySources/MayflowerCompact.php

15. William Bradford, *Bradford's History of "Plimoth Plantation," by William Bradford*, Project Gutenberg ebook, March 29, 2008, www.gutenberg.org/ebooks/24950.

16. Ibid.

17. Ronald Reagan, "Ronald Reagan's Farewell Address," January 11, 1989, text online at Reagan2020.us, http://www.reagan2020.us/speeches/Farewell.asp.

18. John Winthrop, "A Model of Christian Charity," preached aboard the *Arbella* sometime between April and June 1630, available online at The Religious Freedom Page, http://religiousfreedom.lib.virginia.edu/sacred/charity.html.

19. Ibid.

20. Sydney Ahlstrom, *The Religious History of the American People* (New Haven: Yale University Press), 147.

21. Paul Johnson, *A History of the American People* (New York: HarperCollins, 1999), 42.

22. Noll, Hatch, and Marsden, *Search for Christian America*, 39.

23. Ibid., 41.

24. Richard Hofstadter, *Anti-Intellectualism in American Life* (New York: Random House, 1963), 59–60.

25. Ibid., 60.

26. Nye and Morpurgo, *History of the United States*, 51.

27. Paul Johnson, *History of the American People*, 83.

28. A detailed discussion of bundling and its consequences is found in George M. Marsden, *Jonathan Edwards: A Life* (New Haven: Yale University Press, 2003), 130–31.

29. Jonathan Edwards, "Sinners in the Hands of an Angry God," July 8, 1741, text available at the Christian Classics Ethereal Library, http://www.ccel.org/ccel/edwards/sermons.sinners.html.

30. National Humanities Center Resource Toolbox, "Benjamin Franklin on Rev. George Whitefield, 1739," in *Becoming American: The British American Colonies, 1690–1763*, National Humanities Center, http://nationalhumanitiescenter.org/pds/becomingamer/ideas/text2/franklinwhitefield.pdf.

31. Alan Heimert, *Religion and the American Mind* (Cambridge: Harvard University Press, 1966), viii.

32. Noll, Hatch, and Marsden, *Search for Christian America*, 53, 65, and 59, respectively.

33. James Hutson, *Religion and the Founding of the American Republic* (Washington, DC: Library of Congress, 1992), 19.

34. Michael Novak, *On Two Wings: Humble Faith and Common Sense at the American Founding* (San Francisco: Encounter Books, 2001), 129.

35. Thomas S. Kidd, *God of Liberty: A Religious History of the American Revolution* (New York: Basic Books, 2010), 25.

36. Ibid., 76.

37. Cited in ibid., 250.

38. Cited in Rod Gragg, *Forged in Faith: How Faith Shaped the Birth of the Nation 1607–1776* (New York: Howard Books, 2010), 165.

39. Cited in Novak, *On Two Wings*, 23.

40. Cited in Peter Lillback, *George Washington's Sacred Fire* (Bryn Mawr, PA: Providence Forum Press, 2006), 577. Lillback's study of Washington's religious ideas, and specifically his treatment of the question of how serious he was about his Christian faith, is by far the most complete treatment of this question in print.

41. Cited in Novak, *On Two Wings*, 16.

42. Cited in ibid., i.

43. Cited in William J. Federer, *America's God and Country: Encyclopedia of Quotations*, (St. Louis: Amerisearch Inc., 2000), 10.

44. Cited in Gragg, *Forged in Faith*, 143.

45. Cited in ibid., 194.

46. Thomas Jefferson, *Notes on the State of Virginia*, Query XVIII, quoted at "Quotations on the Jefferson Memorial," Monticello.org, http://www.monticello.org/site/jefferson/quotations-jefferson-memorial#Panel_Three.

47. Kidd, *God of Liberty*, 110.

48. Ibid.

49. Cited in Hutson, *Religion and the Founding*, 39.

50. Ibid., 37.

51. Cited in ibid.

52. Cited in ibid.

53. Ibid., 53.

54. Ibid., 54–55.

55. Ibid., 54–56.

56. Cited in ibid., 56.

57. Cited in Peter Lillback, *George Washington's Sacred Fire*, 551.

58. Cited in Hutson, *Religion and the Founding*, 62.

59. James Hutson, *Forgotten Features of the Founding: The Recovery of Religious Themes in the Early American Republic* (Lanham, MD: Lexington Books, 2005), 21–22.

60. Hutson, *Religion and the Founding*, 53.

61. Cited in ibid., 64.

62. Thomas Jefferson, "Letters: The Morals of Jesus, to Dr. Benjamin Rush, with a Syllabus," April 21, 1803. Available online at http://www.positiveatheism.org/hist/jeff1122.htm.

63. The Thomas Jefferson's Monticello website is skeptical about the authenticity of this story, which comes from a Rev. Ethan Allen narrative written in 1857 contained in a string-bound manuscript in the Library of Congress (shelf location MMC-1167; see http://www.monticello.org/site/research-and-collections/no-nation-has-ever-yet-existed-or-been-governed-without-religionquotat). Hutson, however, accepts the probability that the story is true and points out that it was Jefferson who, as Chief Executive, authorized the United States Marine Corps band to attend the church service (*Religion and the Founding*, 96).

64. Hutson, *Religion and the Founding*, 91.

65. Cited in Hutson, ibid., 85.

66. Ibid., 93.

67. Kidd, *God of Liberty*, 39.

68. Cited in Hutson, *Religion and the Founding*, 75.

69. Cited in ibid., 76 (emphasis in original).

70. Cited in ibid., 79–80.

71. "Washington's Farewell Address 1796," The Avalon Project, Lillian Goldman Law Library, Yale University, http://avalon.law.yale.edu/18th_century/washing.asp.

72. Ibid.

73. Cited in Hutson, *Religion and the Founding*, 81.

74. "Inaugural Address of John Adams," The Avalon Project, http://avalon.law.yale.edu/18th_century/adams.asp.

75. Cited in Hutson, *Religion and the Founding*, 82.

76. Ibid., 66.

77. Cited in ibid., 100.

78. Ibid., 101.

79. Cited in ibid., 109.

80. Seymour Martin Lipset, *The First New Nation: The United States in Historical and Comparative Perspective* (New York: W. W. Norton and Company, 1979), 146–50.

81. Alexis de Tocqueville, "Chapter XVII: Principal Causes Maintaining the Democratic Republic—Part III," *Democracy in America*, bk 1. Available online at Project Gutenberg, http://www.gutenberg.org/files/815/815-h/815-h.htm.

82. Abraham Lincoln, "Second Inaugural Address," March 4, 1865, available online at Bartleby.com, http://www.bartleby.com/124/pres32.html.

83. George Bancroft, *History of the United States of America, from the Discovery of the American Continent*, 10 vols. (Boston: Little, Brown, 1854–1878).

84. John Fea, *Was America Founded as a Christian Nation?*, 9.

85. *Church of the Holy Trinity v. United States* (1892), cited in William J. Federer, *America's God and Country: Encyclopedia of Quotations* (St. Louis: Amerisearch, 2000), 71.

86. Ibid., 71–72.

87. David J. Brewer, *The United States a Christian Nation* (Philadelphia: The John C. Winston Company, 1905), 12.

88. "*Church of the Holy Trinity v. United States*," Wikipedia, December 12, 2011, http://en.wikipedia.org/wiki/Church_of_the_Holy_Trinity_v._United_States.

Chapter 4 American Christianity and the Challenge of Modernity

1. Cited in Os Guinness, *The Great Experiment: Faith and Freedom in the American Republic* (Washington, DC: The Trinity Forum, 1999), 14.

2. Ibid., 15.

3. A. Robert Caponigri, *Philosophy from the Romantic Age to the Age of Positivism* (Notre Dame: University of Notre Dame Press, 1971), 71.

4. Bertrand Russell, *History of Western Philosophy* (London: George Allen and Unwin, 1946), 773.

5. Gyorgy Lukacs, *The Young Hegel* (Cambridge: MIT Press, 1975), 4.

6. Georg W. F. Hegel, *Early Theological Writings* (Chicago: University of Chicago Press, 1948), 61.

7. Albert Schweitzer, *The Quest for the Historical Jesus*, 3rd. ed. (London: Adam and Charles Black, 1954), 4.

8. Ibid., 15.

9. Harold Bloom, "The Unpastured Sea: An Introduction to Shelley," in *Ringers in the Tower* (Chicago: University of Chicago, 1971), 99.

10. Cited in S. L. Greenslade, ed., *The Cambridge History of the Bible* vol. 3 (New York: Cambridge University Press, 1963), 274.

11. Cited in David McClellan, *The Young Hegelians and Karl Marx* (London: Macmillan, 1969), 3.

12. Ibid., 52.

13. Cited in *Marx-Engels Gesamtausgabe*, ed. D. Riazonovskii (11 vols.; Frankfurt/Main and Moscow: Marx-Engels Institute, 1927–1935), I, Party 1, Section 2, 263. Subsequent references will refer to this work as *MEGA*.

14. Cited in Karl Lowith, *From Hegel to Nietzsche: The Revolution in Nineteenth Century Thought* (New York: Holt, Rinehart and Winston, 1964), 77.

15. John A. T. Robinson, *Honest to God* (London: SCM Press, 1963), 41.

16. Friedrich Engels, "Ludwig Feuerbach and the End of Classical German Philosophy" in *Marx and Engels: On Religion* (Moscow: Progress Publishers, 1972), 200.

17. Karl Marx and Frederick Engels, *Collected Works*, 50 vols. (London: Lawrence and Wishart, 1975–2004), III, 464.

18. Ludwig Feuerbach, *The Essence of Christianity*, trans. George Eliot (New York: Harper and Row, 1957), 140 (emphasis in original).

19. Karl Marx, *Early Writings* (Harmondsworth, England: Penguin Books, 1975), 243–44 (italics in original).

20. Julie S. Reuben, *The Making of the Modern University* (Chicago: University of Chicago Press, 1996), 81.

21. "Prejudice of Americans towards Mormons and Evangelicals," Ontario Consultants on Religious Tolerance, 2007, www.religioustolerance.org/evanintol.htm.

22. George M. Marsden, *The Soul of the American University* (New York and Oxford: Oxford University Press, 1994), 39.

23. Ibid., 41.

24. See ibid., 92–93, for a detailed account of the influence on American education of the common sense philosophy.

25. Ibid., 5.

26. Ibid., 87.

27. Cited in ibid., 89.

28. Ibid., 104–5.

29. Cited in ibid., 106–7.

30. Cited in ibid., 107.

31. Cited in ibid., 103.

32. Ibid., 115.

33. Cited in ibid.

34. Cited in Reuben, *Making of the Modern University*, 121.

35. Susan Jacoby, *Freethinkers: A History of American Secularism* (New York: Henry Holt, 2004), 151.

36. Reuben, *Making of the Modern University*, 88–89.

37. Margaret Sanger, *The Pivot of Civilization*, available online at Project Gutenberg, www.gutenberg.org/ebooks/1689.

38. Charles Darwin, *The Descent of Man*, in Clifton Fadiman, Philip W. Goetz, eds., *Great Books of the Western World*, vol. 49 (Chicago: Encyclopedia Britannica, 1993), 326.

39. Sanger, *Pivot of Civilization*.

40. Cited in Marsden, *Soul of the American University*, 25.

41. Cited in ibid., 130.

42. Cited in Alister McGrath, *The Twilight of Atheism* (New York: Doubleday, 2004), 99.

43. Marsden, *Soul of the American University*, 255.

44. Cited in ibid., 255.

45. Cited in Reuben, *Making of the Modern University*, 68.

46. Cited in Marsden, *Soul of the American University*, 119.

47. Ibid.

48. Cited in Reuben, *Making of the Modern University*, 59.

49. Cited in Marsden, *Soul of the American University*, 203.

50. Cited in ibid., 54.

51. Cited in ibid., 77.

52. Cited in Reuben, *Making of the Modern University*, 130–31.

53. Ibid., 132.

54. Marsden, *Soul of the American University*, 292–93.

55. Edward J. Larson and Larry Witham, "Leading Scientists Still Reject God," *Nature* 394, no. 6691 (1998): 313. Available online at http://www.stephenjaygould.org/ctrl/news/file002.html.

56. Marsden, *Soul of the American University*, 294.

57. Ronald L. Numbers, *Darwinism Comes to America* (Cambridge: Harvard University Press, 1998), 87.

58. Cited in Alister McGrath, *Twilight of Atheism*, 76.

59. Tom Brokaw, *The Greatest Generation* (New York: Random House, 2004).

60. Templeton appears to have actually had a vision of heaven (to which presumably he was going to be welcome, despite his apostasy) just before his death in 2001. See David Aikman, *Billy Graham: His Life and Influence* (Nashville: Thomas Nelson, 2007), 64.

61. See especially Laura Hillenbrand, *Unbroken: A World War II Story of Survival, Resilience, and Redemption* (New York: Random House, 2010).

62. Cited in Aikman, *Billy Graham: His Life and Influence*, 186.

63. Cited in Michael S. Horton, "Beyond Culture Wars," *Modern Reformation* 2, no. 3 (May/June 1993): 1–4. Available online at http://www.modernreformation.org/default.php?page=articledisplay&var1=ArtRead&var2=831&var3=main.

64. Roger Kimball, *The Long March: How the Cultural Revolution of the 1960s Changed America* (San Francisco: Encounter Books, 2000), 27.

65. Robert Bork, *Slouching Towards Gomorrah* (San Francisco: HarperPerennial, 1997), 53.

66. Students for a Democratic Society, "Port Huron Statement of the Students for a Democratic Society," June 1962, http://www.h-net.org/~hst306/documents/huron.html.

67. Bork, *Slouching Towards Gomorrah*, 27.

68. George Orwell, *1984* (New York: Penguin, 1949), 269.

69. See the Pennsylvania State University study "Living Together before Marriage: Now Common but Still Risky," August 3, 2003, http://live.psu.edu/story/3682.

Chapter 5 Countertrends

1. Christopher Dawson, *Religion and the Rise of Western Culture* (Garden City, NY: Image Books, 1991).

2. "Church History Timeline: 1807, William Wilberforce," Christianity.com, http://www.christianity.com/ChurchHistory/11630357/.

3. Peter L. Berger, ed., *The Desecularization of the World* (Washington, DC: Ethics and Public Policy Center and Eerdmans, 1999), 2.

4. Ibid., 11–12.

5. Ibid., 4.

6. Ibid., 2–3.

7. Quotes here and above are from Hunter Baker, *The End of Secularism* (Wheaton: Crossway Books, 2009), 122.

8. The Chinese government, in accordance with its constitution, permits religious worship in China but only under strict government supervision. A government-

appointed umbrella group, the Three-Self Patriotic Movement, oversees all officially "open" Protestant churches in China's cities, but it refuses to recognize the existence of millions of Christians who prefer to worship in "house churches" that are outside the government purview. The population of house-church Christians is probably three times as large as the Christians who attend only Three-Self churches. Conservatively, house-church Christians may number about sixty million, though some Chinese estimate the number to be closer to twice that figure. In one of the most astonishing displays of "the emperor has no clothes" syndrome ever displayed by a large and powerful government, the Chinese government refuses to admit that house churches exist. In early 2011, a house church in Beijing composed of precisely the same kind of upscale professionals as described in *God Is Back* suffered serious and ongoing harassment because it refused to operate under the control of the TSPM.

9. John Micklethwait and Adrian Wooldridge, *God Is Back* (New York: Penguin, 2009), 3.

10. Michele A. Vu, "Chinese Government Attributes Western Success to Christianity," *Christian Post*, May 19, 2011, http://au.christiantoday.com/article/chinese-government-attributes-western-success-to-christianity/11081.htm.

11. Cited in David Aikman, *Jesus in Beijing: How Christianity Is Transforming China and Changing the Global Balance of Power* (Washington, DC: Regnery, 2003), 5.

12. See Vu, "Chinese Government Attributes Western Success to Christianity."

13. Quentin Smith, "The Metaphilosophy of Naturalism," *PHILO* 4, no. 2 (2001), http://www.philoonline.org/library/smith_4_2.htm.

14. "Getting the Most out of College," InterVarsity Christian Fellowship, news release, September 2, 2011, http://www.intervarsity.org/news/getting-most-out-college.

15. See www.Luke18project.com.

16. See "About 24-7," http://www.24-7prayer.com/about/what.

17. Jaeson Ma, *The Blueprint: A Revolutionary Plan to Plant Missional Communities on Campus* (Ventura, CA: Regal Books, 2007), 102 (emphasis in original).

18. Jaeson Ma, interview with the author, December 2, 2011.

19. Matt Bennett, "The Mission and Vision of Christian Union," Christian Union, http://involve.christian-union.org/site/PageServer?pagename=CUMission.

20. Eileen Scott, "Can We Really Change the World? Ivy League Congress on Faith and Action Draws 380 Students," Christian Union, September 23, 2011, http://involve.christian-union.org/site/News2?page=NewsArticle&id=8202&security=1&news_iv_ctrl=-1.

21. John Piper, *Desiring God: Meditations of a Christian Hedonist* (Colorado Springs: Multnomah Books, 1986).

22. "About Us," Desiring God, 2012, http://www.desiringgod.org/about.

23. John Piper, telephone interview with the author, June 30, 2011.

24. Molly Worthern, "Who Would Jesus Smack Down?" *New York Times*, January 6, 2009, http://www.nytimes.com/2009/01/11/magazine/11punk-t.html?pagewanted=all.

25. Richard Land, telephone interview with the author, August 19, 2011.

26. T. D. Jakes, telephone interview with the author, September 28, 2011.

27. Franklin Graham, telephone interview with the author, September 8, 2011.

28. Loren Cunningham, interview with the author, September 13, 2011.

29. Alex Harris and Jeremy Siblerud, interviews with the author at Patrick Henry College, September 9, 2011.

30. Global Leadership Summit 2010, Willow Creek Church, South Barrington, Illinois, http://www.willowcreek.com/wca_prodsb.asp?invtid=PR34770.

31. "Extended Interview: Zhao Xiao," *Frontline World: Jesus in China*, original airdate June 24, 2008, http://www.pbs.org/frontlineworld/stories/china_705/interview/xiao.html.

32. Cited in Micklethwait and Wooldridge, *God Is Back*, 9.

David Aikman is an award-winning print and broadcast journalist, a bestselling author, and a foreign affairs commentator based in the Washington, DC, area. His wide-ranging professional achievements include a twenty-three-year career at *Time* magazine and twelve books. He has appeared as a commentator and guest on all the major news networks, including NBC, ABC, CNN, FOX News, and the BBC, and his editorials regularly air on radio stations across the United States. He lives in Virginia. If you would like to learn more about this book and about David or to receive free samples of his other books, please visit www.davidaikman.com, www.onenationwithout.com, or www.kidnappedingaza.com.